OTTERS

Liz Laidler

OTTERS
IN BRITAIN

DAVID & CHARLES

Newton Abbot   London   North Pomfret (Vt)

Page 2
Upright tripod posture, using hind legs and tail to balance—all the better to see and hear

British Library Cataloguing in Publication Data

Laidler, Liz
    Otters in Britain—(British mammals; 2)
    1. Otters
    I. Title   II. Series
    599.74′ 447   QL737.C25

    ISBN 0-7153-8069-9

Typeset by Typesetters (Birmingham) Ltd
and printed in Great Britain
by Ebenezer Baylis & Son Ltd, Worcester
for David & Charles (Publishers) Limited
Brunel House   Newton Abbot   Devon

Published in the United States of America
by David & Charles Inc
North Pomfret   Vermont 05053   USA

Contents

The Brown diving otter is no longer gliding
Beneath the fring'd banks of the cool valley rill
Nor bittern is calling, not curlew is hiding,
Nor badger is hous'd in the cleft of the hill.

Thomas Lister, 1853
Tributary Ode to Stainborough

1
Portrait of an Otter

There can't be many animals around who can claim the privilege of a
saint's blessing and holy patronage, but the otter is one of the chosen
few. It was good St Cuthbert of Northumberland who bestowed his
favour on otters and as Gavin Maxwell observed in his famous book
Ring of Bright Water, St Cuthbert must have been a man with the
power of enlightened discrimination for the otter is surely one of the
most graceful and intelligent of mammals, a creature worthy of special
attention and saintly care.

The story goes that St Cuthbert was in the habit of forgoing his
sleep and going out at night to pray, while the other monks slept in
their cells. One night a brother from the abbey at Coldringham
followed him to find out where the great man went and what he did
on his long nightly sojourns. The peeping Tom saw St Cuthbert walk
down to the sea and wade into the water up to his shoulders, chanting
all the while. Towards dawn, the saint came back out and prayed on
the beach. What followed was like a strange dream, more appropriate
to the animal-loving St Francis of Assisi than to a pagan-braving
missionary like St Cuthbert. The spy saw two 'four-footed beasts'
emerge from the water and prostrate themselves before the berobed
figure, 'warming his feet with pantings, and trying to dry them with
their fur'. After having been blessed by the saint, the pair of otters
returned to the water and St Cuthbert got back to the abbey in time
for the six o'clock service.

The otters may well have been full of the milk of Christian
kindness, intending to towel the saint's feet dry, but from Maxwell's
experiences of his own pet otters, it was probably more a case of trying
to get dry themselves and looking upon their human friend as an
obliging rubbing post. Either way St Cuthbert was obviously an

7

exceptional man in being befriended by two wild otters in this way. Untamed otters are extremely shy animals with very sensitive habits and confine their activities to the hours of darkness.

So seldom was the otter seen on land or swimming at the surface of river or lake that, centuries ago, people thought it was a large fish. But as any first-former today will tell you, the otter is as different from a fish as an elephant from an insect. Its closest relatives include stoats, weasels, mink, martens, badgers, tayras and wolverines—the group of mammals known as mustelids. The members of this zoological family are all characterised by having scent glands; they vary widely in size, from the 8 inch (20cm) weasel to the 7ft (over 2m) long giant otter of South America, and they live in just about every kind of niche there is. Tayras live in trees, badgers retreat into setts and otters dwell on land and water.

St Cuthbert's otter, the European or common otter, *Lutra lutra*, inhabits the streams, rivers, lakes, marshes and coasts of Britain and Ireland and the vast continental expanse of Europe and Asia. Its range extends from as far north as the Arctic Circle to northern India and Tibet, through the eastern islands of Sri Lanka, Java and Japan, westwards to Morocco and Algeria in Africa. Strangely enough it is absent from the Mediterranean islands, the otters in Sicily and Corfu having been introduced. Except in India, the home of *Lutrogale perspicillata*, and Sumatra and the nearby islands where *Lutra lutra sumatrana* and *Amblonyx cinerea* are also found, the European otter does not share its range with any other otter species. Its vast distribution has encouraged the evolution of a number of sub-species or races found mostly in Asia around the Himalayas and beyond.

Unfortunately, the distribution of the European otter today is but a shadow of what it was. The last thirty years or so have seen changes in land-use policies, a massive spread of recreational activities and pollution of rivers and lakes. The disturbance effect on otter populations has been enormous and has permanently wiped out the species in some areas. Whereas in the old days there used to be otters wherever there were watercourses (fresh and salt) and sufficient tree and bush cover to ensure privacy, today even where these two basic requirements still exist, otters may be absent. The species has been ousted from its favourite habitats as well as from more marginal ones

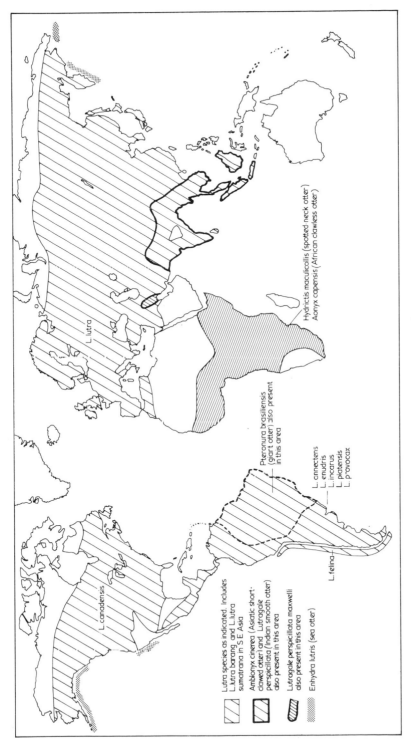

1 World distribution of otter species

Legend:

Lutra species as indicated. Includes L.lutra barang and L.lutra sumatrana in S.E.Asia

Amblonyx cinerea (Asiatic short-clawed otter) and Lutrogale perspicillata (Indian smooth otter) also present in this area

Lutrogale perspicillata maxwelli also present in this area

Enhydra lutris (sea otter)

L. canadensis

L. lutra

Pteronura brasiliensis (giant otter) also present in this area

Hydrictis maculicollis (spotted-neck otter)
Aonyx capensis (African clawless otter)

L. annectens
L. enudris
L. incarus
L. platensis
L. provocax

L. felina

at the busy hands of progressive man. In Britain, it was once distributed widely, over a variety of different habitats, but with its abandonment of many river systems, marshlands and coastlines, the extent of its range has shrunk to about one-third of what it used to be. The only regions where the otter exists in anything like its optimum density are Scotland and north Wales.

'The otter represents the most elegant solution to the problem of constructing an amphibious carnivore that nature has so far effected,' wrote Bjorn Kurten, and the animal is indeed the essence of suppleness. Its head is as wide as it is long and leads onto a short, compact neck so that an otter swimming underwater has the smooth contours of a bullet; the long sinuous body ends in a thick tapering tail. Many people who have kept otters have remarked on the apparent bonelessness of the body, its ability to bend backwards or forwards, yoga-fashion, so that nose touches tail. There is no special reason for this, just that the vertebrae are fairly loosely articulated with one another, rather like those of a double-jointed dancer.

Not everyone recognised the otter as a symbol of grace and beauty. There was the odd jaundice-eyed bigot who failed to discern anything attractive in this Olympian of swimmers. The well-known French naturalist G. L. Buffon assailed the poor creature with unconstrained criticisms of its physical appearance. For him, otter cubs had 'badly made' heads with low-placed ears and tiny eyes, giving them an altogether 'gloomy expression'. Anyone could see, too, that their movements were awkward and their 'mechanical and continual' cries were likewise cause for complaint. It is hard to believe that such a delightful creature could elicit such obloquy, but there is comfort in knowing that the Buffons of this world are few.

The world's smallest otter is the clawless otter of the East Indies which is usually less than 3ft (1 metre) long, while at the other end of the scale is the South American giant otter, which measures more than twice this length. Adult European otters are rather larger than the East Indian species—about 3-4ft long from nose to tail end, the tail itself exceeding half the length of the head and body put together. Male otters, or dog otters as they are called, are appreciably longer and heavier than bitches, weighing an average of 24lb (11kg) as opposed to 16lb (7kg) or so for the females. Although these measurements are the

Pair of otters feeding - showing the white patches on cheeks and throat

norm, much larger heavier specimens have been recorded. In Westmorland in 1917 the biggest female on record was caught; measuring a total of 4½ft and tipping the scales at 27.75lb (12.7kg). In December 1952, a Scottish newspaper claimed that a dog otter of 'almost 60lb' had been killed in Caithness. No mention was made of its length but it could have been as much as 6ft (2m) since earlier writers mention male otters that long and an anonymous correspondent in *The Field* records in 1860 how on several occasions he met with giant-size otter footprints near the mouth of the Perry, a mile below Mumfordbridge. Apart from being heavier and slightly longer than bitches, dog otters can be distinguished by their thicker necks and broader muzzles.

The otter's thick, glossy coat is usually chestnut-brown on the back and pale on the underside, with white patches on the cheeks and throat. But the intensity of the brown can vary considerably from place to place and from season to season, graduating through a spectrum of grey to deep red-brown or almost black. Southern believes that the darkest, thickest pelage is acquired in winter after the autumn moult. But this begs the question of whether there is a second moult every year. It is generally believed that the otter undergoes a slow change of coat in autumn, but no one has actually seen it happen in spring. It may be that the winter coat simply wears thin over the spring and summer, to be replaced again in autumn. The variation of coat colour according to locality has attracted considerably more study: Dadd, for example, describes the Irish population of otters as possessing a definitely darker coat than the British population, almost black on the upper side and with less white on the throat. He proposes that Irish otters should be regarded as a distinct sub-species or race because of this difference. Earlier authors in fact tried to establish the otter in Ireland as actually a separate species, not merely a sub-species, though as well as coat colour they listed other small differences in physical appearance to justify their claim.

A small proportion of melanic and albino individuals occur in many animal populations the world over, and the European otter is no exception. Albinos, the individuals with a completely white coat and pink eyes, have no melanin in the pigment cells of their skin—human albinos cannot tan, no matter how long they stay out in the sun! Judging by the number of mainly nineteenth-century accounts, albinism is, or was, fairly common in the European otter. White or cream coloured otters have been seen in Ireland in the River Shannon, in the River Aln in Northumberland and off the shores of the Hebrides. Strangely enough, an area along the west coast of Scotland, in the neighbourhood of Mull, Islay and Jura, was inhabited by a fairly large group of albino otters. It is difficult to say what proportion of the local otter population these white forms represented because several of the stories are probably repeats of one another, but the sightings do suggest a greater than usual number of albino individuals. In March 1903, Kirk tells of a cream-coloured otter having been captured at Kildaton in Islay, a male weighing 17¾lb (around 8kg), and this was just one of at least four albino otters bagged in or around Islay. Another one was killed at Torosay Castle on the Isle of Mull. It seems that white otters were selectively killed because they were rare—and probably because they stood out a mile—and yet despite the shootings, all-white otters were still being spotted off the west coast of Argyll and in Tongland as recently as the 1950s and 60s.

Otters with white spots have also featured in the literature on the European otter but the authenticity of many of them, particularly of mounted specimens or preserved skins, must be questioned if the following esoteric secret of 1862 is anything to go by:

First catch an umber-brown otter . . . stuff him, set him in a shop window where the scorching rays of the sun will bleach him white in the course of 3 or 4 years (sousing him occasionally in his native element will cause him to bleach sooner and come out pure white); shorter time makes him cream colour. If he is to be ticked like a pointer, keep him from the sun, wrapped in paper, and cut a few holes in the paper; apply nitric or other acid to turn his hair white—any chemist can do this. If he is to be zebraised (ie, given stripes like a zebra!), wind round him some lead foil in stripes, or hoop him up with old crinoline, before he undergoes bleaching. . . .

It seems that this sort of tampering with nature was a lucrative business and the above recipe makes the transformation sound as easy as baking cakes on a Sunday. Still, there *was* such a thing as a real spotted otter and about half a dozen sightings and catches of these have been published. An interesting myth about spotted otters was alive in Scotland in the early 1800s. Apparently, the Scottish 'vulgar', the lower classes, believed that an otter spotted with white was the king or leader of a group of otters. If one was killed a man or some other animal would die simultaneously. But perversely enough, if a skin was obtained (presumably at the expense of a human life), it made an effective medicament against infection and was a coveted talisman for ensuring the safety of warriors and mariners.

The European otter does not have a melanic form. There has been the odd tale of a black otter but an otter briefly glimpsed in the wild can so easily be mistaken as being black. The glossy fur is a good reflector of adjacent colours, even when wet, and the wetness itself gives the coat a darker appearance.

It takes ingenuity and no small degree of technology to protect humans from the cold and wet but the otter has not had to think about it. Nature has provided this sleek swimmer with a thick layer

2 Grooming postures: (A) biting the thigh fur; (B) cleaning the anal and genital area; (C) cleaning a forepaw; (D) rubbing and scratching the back; (E) nibbling and licking the chest; (F) rubbing and scratching the stomach and chest (*Pippa Holkham*)

of subcutaneous fat and a waterproof coat of superb construction. So efficient is the otter's 'sweater' that man has for centuries deprived the animal of it for his own use. The secret of an otter's pelt is its double-layer composition. There is an under layer of fine, dense fur protected and almost completely hidden by an outer covering of longer, stiffer

14

guard-hairs which are kept well oiled to repel water. So dense is the underfur that even if the hairs are forcibly parted the skin does not show through. The glossy guard-hairs are greyish-white at the roots and deep brown at the extremities and are about twice as long (25mm or nearly an inch) as the soft off-white underhairs. The thickness of an otter pelt generally depends on the latitude from which the animal comes and European otters in Siberia, for example, have denser coats than their British counterparts.

The fur protects its owner from the cold by trapping a layer of insulating air, about a quarter of an inch thick, among the close-packed underhairs. When the otter climbs out of the water onto the bank, the water runs off the waterproof guard hairs, causing them to aggregate into small bunches. Each bunch tapers to a tip giving the animal a characteristic spiky appearance. Nicole Duplaix, who made a study of various otter species in captivity, found that if an otter's coat did not form spikes after coming out of the water, the coat was in poor condition and the animal likely to catch pneumonia. But even when the otter is in good shape it never remains in the water for more than about half an hour at a time, and if prevented from landing the poor creature will become chilled and start to shiver. It then takes a long session of meticulous rubbing and grooming to get the fur dry

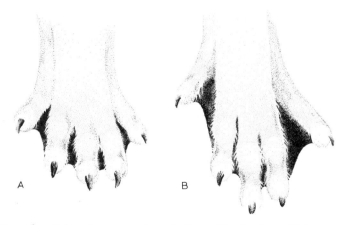

3   Otter feet (left), showing webs and claws. The forefoot (A) is shorter than the hindfoot (B), and the thumb is positioned further forward than the big toe (*Pippa Holkham*)

Drying off

Close up of the spiky effect of wet otter fur

again. This situation often occurs during otter hunts when the animal tries to hide from its pursuers. No doubt its distressed condition makes the final capture easier for the hunters.

The common otter conforms to the anatomical blueprint of all otters in having short legs and webbed feet. There are five toes on each foot and they bear sharp, curved claws which can grip fish securely and make climbing slippery banks easier. Not all otter species have webs between their digits. The clawless otters of Africa and south-east Asia lack any sign of skin there and this gives the fingers remarkable

Trotting

Floating backwards
among the ice
(Beverley Trowbridge)

dexterity and freedom of movement. The muscular tail, or rudder,
slightly horizontally flattened near its base, is the means by which the
otter moves and steers in water. In some specimens, the tip is quite
bare and some country folk reckoned this was because the otter used it
to push fish out from behind rocks. But it is more likely due to close
encounters with a playmate's toothy arsenal: observations on captive
otters show that both adults and cubs have a penchant for nipping each
other's tails during play.

It is in the water that the otter is at its most confident, a sleek form

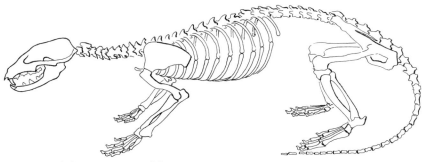

4   Otter skeleton (*Pippa Holkham*)

of power and grace. Forward thrust is provided by beating the tail up and down like the fluke of a dolphin or whale, the hind legs being manipulated to aid steering. The only time the forelegs disengage from the smooth, bud-like contour is when a quick burst of speed is needed. The tail is also handy as a third leg or prop when the otter stands erect in shallow water or on land the better to hear, smell and see some interesting object. I have also seen this weasel-like trait in giant otters while studying them in Guyana. Wild individuals as well as the adult female in the local zoo have raised themselves erect whenever a sight or sound attracted their attention from a distance. At top speed, an otter swimming underwater can push 7-9 miles (11-14km) per hour but such intense exertion is like doing the 100-metre sprint and can only be kept up for short periods. Great energy is also expended when otters engage in a quick succession of dolphin-like leaps but they only occasionally do this when playing or courting. It is more usual for an otter to travel at a rather calmer pace, in a series of smooth, shallow dives, surfacing every fifteen seconds or so to breathe. Deep diving is used in fishing: the head is pointed straight down at the same time as the hind legs are kicked backwards, shooting the animal into the depths. The body curves into a question mark on the surface and all you see is a dark hump as rudder follows body through the arc. Many a time the black form of an otter's back has fooled those of us who have spent long hours in the cold and wet waiting to catch a glimpse of the Loch Ness monster.

Submerged, otters can maintain an almost vertical position by treading water with their hind paws, a stance which allows the head and neck to be raised out of the water. Many observers have remarked how silently and with the merest of ripples an otter can disappear beneath the surface of the water when in this position, an obvious advantage when an unnoticed exit is required. Like humans, otters rise naturally to the surface if they stop swimming and find no difficulty in floating belly upwards or downwards. Philip Wayre, founder and honorary director of the Otter Trust in Suffolk, found that many of his captive otters would float on their stomachs with heads just submerged in order to size up the food situation down below—or perhaps they did it to see what an aqualunged human looks like underwater!

On land, otters transport themselves more awkwardly though, surprisingly enough, they can reach greater speeds than in water—as much as 15 or more miles (24-25km) an hour. When walking the head and neck are held low with the hips and lower back arched up, the tail extending straight behind and kept just above the ground. The wedge shape is a consequence of the back legs being twice as long as the front

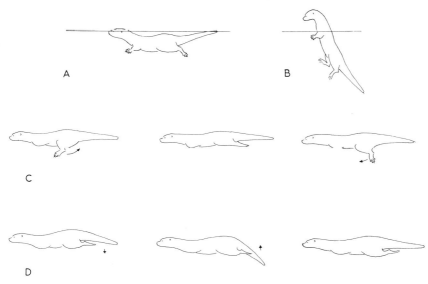

5   Otter locomotion in water: (A) afloat, with eyes, ears and nostrils above water; (B) 'periscoping', treading water to raise head and chest; (C) paddling, using hind-limb movements, with power, glide and recovery phases; (D) fast swimming, using back and tail movements (*Pippa Holkham*)

On all fours prior to upright stance—a good view of webbed feet

ones. Moving together, the fore- and hind-limb feet of one side alternate with those of the opposite side but the set-up changes during galloping (bounding), the gait the otter uses when it wants to travel at top speed over land. The forefeet now move together as one, as the back arches, alternating with the hind pair which provide the thrust when the back straightens. The result is ungainly, the back humping into the air and extending repetitively. Two men in a snowmobile once followed a North American otter for several minutes over hard-packed snow. The otter kept up a cracking pace which the men estimated from their speedometer as somewhere between 15 and 18 miles (24-29km) per hour. No one has ever been able to time a European otter in the same way but the two species have many similarities and it therefore seems likely that our native otter could make the same speed when flat out. Of the many different kinds of surface otters will travel on during their lifetime, snow is without doubt the most pleasurable. It lends an exhilarating helping hand by providing a slippery surface on which they can slide and run alternately. Pushing off with their back legs, the otters ski on their stomachs for 10-20ft (3-6m) before launching into another gallop. During each slide, the front legs are folded back onto the chest like two penknife blades tucked out of the way. The gentlest of slopes is put to use and even level surfaces are often skated on, the propulsion being mustered in this case by side-to-side flexion of the body.

The head of the otter is an efficient computer. The components are all there for receiving and processing information from the outside world. Eyes, ears, nose and whiskers do the receiving while the pear-sized brain takes care of the processing. The processor's casing, the skull, unfortunately has only a thin roof and is no match against a hunter's bludgeon. The eyes and nostrils are positioned well on top of the head so that the otter can still breathe and look around while the rest of its body is submerged. An upturned nose is an invaluable adaptation in animals which spend much of their time immersed at the water's surface, such as frogs, crocodiles and hippos. It does have the disadvantage, however, of making objects directly in front of the face difficult to see. Neal discovered this when feeding small scraps on the

Surface swimming, with ears, eyes and nose above water (*Angela Potter*)

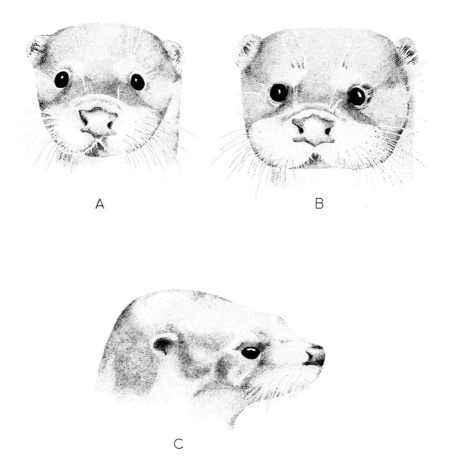

A   B

C

6 Head of the otter, showing heavily whiskered face. (A) female; (B) male, with broader, thicker muzzle; (C) side view—note forward-facing eyes on a level with nose and ears (*Pippa Holkham*)

lawn to an otter cub he was rearing. It would frequently overshoot the mark and had to fall back on smell for guidance.

Otters are of course air-breathing creatures, not fish, and a valvular action automatically closes their nostrils on submersion. This enables them to drink with their heads completely underwater, which is in fact their normal practice, for they do not lap like a cat or dog. In describing the vicissitudes of home-raising two young otter cubs called Kate and Lucy, Wayre recounts how they conformed to this method of imbibing liquid by plunging their heads into a firmly held mug and sucking up with mighty gurgles. The process continued smoothly until they had quenched their thirst. Then Lucy would dip her snout into the water as if for a final suck but instead take it upon herself to blow out hard, spraying everyone in the kitchen in cold, atomised droplets. And when an otter blows it blows. It has a large lung capacity which allows it to hold its breath for as long as four minutes and swim underwater for a quarter of a mile or more without surfacing.

The shape and hairiness of an otter's nose is different for every species and scientists have found it a useful criterion for classification. For the common otter, the hairless black portion is smaller than most —about half an inch wide and two-thirds of an inch long. The North American otter is the only otter species with a totally hairless rhinarium while that of the giant otter of South America is unique in being completely covered in hair.

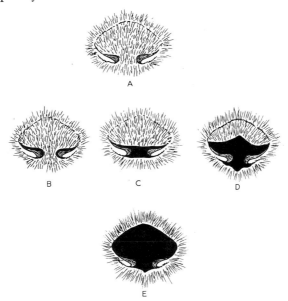

7 Progressive enlargement of the hairless part of the nose among different otter species. Otter species near the equator are hairier than those in temperate regions: (A) *Pteronura brasiliensis*; (B) *Lutra Lutra sumatrana*; (C) *Lutra felina*; (D) *Lutra lutra*; (E) *Lutra canadensis* (*After J. A. Davis*)

Profile of an otter (*Beverley Trowbridge*)

The otter's small, rounded ears offer little resistance to water flow because they have the same reflex response as the nostrils: the little flaps of furred skin which make up the ear pinnae press over the openings as soon as the water rises over them. The eyes, on the other hand, remain completely open underwater and otters actually see better in water than out of it. Only during sleep or rest periods are the eyes closed. Surprisingly, no one seems sure whether the European otter possesses a nictitating membrane—that transparent second eyelid that gives extra protection to the cornea in many amphibia, reptiles and birds—in spite of all the pets that have been raised under close supervision. Several naturalists claim that it does, but Harris, a scientist knowledgeable in otters, feels that while there seems to be 'a protective membrane of some sort' covering each eyeball, he has never seen it blink, as nictitating membranes do.

Cats, dogs and otters all have at least one obvious feature in common—a facial forest of stiff, touch-sensitive whiskers or vibrissae on their muzzles. In the common otter, they are longer and far more prolific than in a cat or dog, forming a conspicuous moustache and beard. The main group emerges from either side of the snout above the lips and from the throat. There are smaller sprays behind each corner of the mouth, a few bristles that form eyebrows of a sort and an elbow tuft on each foreleg. On an adult male skin from Norfolk, Harris also found three or four stalks on the outer point of each wrist. The flesh in which the whiskers are embedded is well endowed with nerve pads which are immediately activated when the whiskers come in contact with anything, be it the edge of the bank or vibrations in the water; the signal is relayed to the brain, which then 'tells' the otter that it is feeling something. This fine system enables an otter to judge distances from the river bottom in poor light conditions or in muddy water when the visibility is poor. It must also help in detecting and catching a meal through the small currents set up by moving prey.

Like a pair of dressmaker's pinking scissors is perhaps the best way to describe a set of otter teeth in action. The dentition is adapted for crushing bones and cutting flesh. A pair of long, backwardly curved canine teeth on each jaw are used to impale the prey and to grip it while the otter chews with its large back teeth. The small, pointed projections on these, the tubercles, simultaneously mince flesh and grind bones and other hard parts. Chewing is important to an otter if it is to avoid choking on some tasty morsel, because its gullet is a small tube barely half an inch in diameter. On either side of the upper jaw are three incisors, one canine, four premolars and one molar. The lower jaw bears the same number of incisors and canines but three premolars and two molars. The bottom jaw does not move sideways, only up and down, but this limitation is of no account to the otter because the muscles which move the lower jaw provide power enough to take care of any fish or mammal bone. Otters show their mammalian heritage by having a set of milk teeth during the early stages of life which are later replaced by a permanent set.

Even without assault by that most fearsome of human indulgences, sugar, otter teeth are plagued with as much decay as our own. This has been found in captive animals, particularly adults, which have been fed much the same type of diet as they would get in the wild. Although the teeth wear with age—the first signs of wearing occurring around the third year of life—it is not possible to assess how old an otter is by looking at its teeth. The degree of tooth erosion varies individually according to an animal's particular experiences and not on any chronological scale as in squirrels. For example, Harris describes how wild otters caught in a trap frequently do terrible damage to their teeth by trying to extricate themselves from their metal prison.

An otter's scent glands are a vital part of its communication system. Embedded in the muscle of the anal region, the two glands are each no bigger than a large marble and are found in both dogs and bitches. They are 'perfume factories', engaged in full-time production of strong-smelling scent. Small quantities of the liquid (brown and oily in adults, white and more fluid in young otters) enter the anus through two small tubes and are deposited on various objects to mark the otter's territory. Sudden fear will also stimulate the glands to release their fluid, in the same way as a badly frightened man might wet himself. In this situation of heightened excitement, the scent is ejected forcibly, though not in a jet like a skunk. Skunks can squirt their notorious scent 4 metres towards a threatening target, the action being defensive rather than just a consequence of sudden alarm.

Dog otters have what is known rather coyly in the scientific world as an *os penis* or bacculum. It is simply a bone which supports the penis and is found only in certain mammals. Penile bones used to be coveted by otter hunters for satisfying the twin desires of adornment and trophy. The slender bones were made into tie pins, watch chains and brooches. The size of the *os penis* depends on the age of the animal and scientists have used this fact to place male otters, bears, dogs, badgers, pine-martens and other mammals that have one into various age groupings: young, juvenile, sub-adult and adult. The older the otter, the larger and heavier the *os penis*, the biggest ever recorded being 2½ inches (63.5mm) long and ¾ inch (19.05mm) in diameter. Two Canadian scientists, Hooper and Ostenson, have used another method to age otters of both sexes. They looked at the joints, or sutures, between the skull bones and measured the extent to which they had grown together. In old otters the sutures had fused, whereas in younger individuals the gaps were still obvious. Both methods are, of course, only useful on dead animals and therefore of limited application.

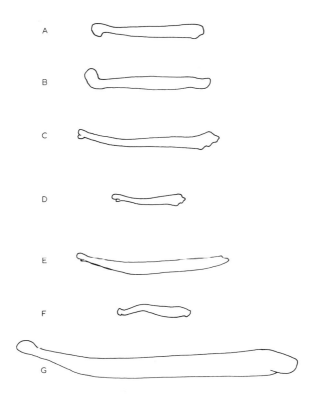

8 Bacculas of adult otter species, outer end on the left, drawn half actual size: (A) *Lutra lutra*; (B) *Lutra canadensis anectens*; (C) *Lutragale perspicillata*; (D) *Amblonyx cinerea*; (E) *Hydrictis maculicollis*; (F) *Pteronura brasiliensis*; (G) *Enhydra lutris* (*After J. A. Davis*)

Penile bones are quite fragile and are prone to fracture under natural conditions but it is difficult to see how these injuries are sustained. Scientists and naturalists have examined many specimens of the European otter killed by man for one reason or another and found large numbers with broken penile bones. One favourite explanation is that such injuries result from rival males fighting among themselves at mating time. But there is no hard evidence to support this belief and two arguments against it. First, the European otter does not have a specific mating season in which neighbouring males would become simultaneously aggressive, and secondly, it hardly seems likely that a species which meticulously endeavours to avoid contact with neighbouring males should contain so many 'injured soldiers'. Surely too a fight in which adversaries manage to gain access to an organ as remote as the penis (the common otter's being encased in the abdominal skin when not erect) would also inflict noticeable scars in other more vulnerable parts of the body, such as the neck and shoulders. Aside from shot-gun scars, old wounds have never been reported in the numerous dead otters and skins that have been examined over the years. Who knows, perhaps bacculum fracture occurs during mating!

Describing the physical features of an animal is only a very small part of getting to know the creature—the anatomical hardware of the species. There is a great deal more to be learnt about what the animal actually does and how it orders its life.

2
Nomad or Landowner?

The otter's vagrant habits claimed the attention of the old Norsemen, who called it 'Tarka', the 'Water Wanderer', implying that it was a gipsy with no fixed address, roaming from one stretch of water to another. This is far from the truth. In 1958 a Swedish biologist, Sam Erlinge, undertook an eight-year study of the European otter in his native land. He found that otters confined their movements, extensive as they were, to restricted areas and that because these home ranges were defended by the occupants against other competing otters, they were in fact territories. The European otter is not a nomad as the Vikings believed; it is a landowner, and as such joins the serried ranks of such beasts as lions, stoats, and foxes.

Not all animals are territorial. Probably as many as one-third of the world's species do not have territories at any time of year. Some creatures, such as army ants, eels and red deer, simply feed and breed in an area without entering into *territorial* displays of any kind. This may surprise some people because it is a fact often omitted in popular wildlife books and films—fights and fantastic I-am-the-boss displays are after all more exciting than humdrum co-existence.

Erlinge was not the first to declare the European otter territorial; at least eight scientists, writing in the three decades prior to the 1960s, had suspected it. But he was the first to support his claim with firm field evidence and the first to obtain detailed information on the size, upkeep and use of otter territories. In Sherlock Holmes fashion, he followed the footprints, pathways, droppings (spraint) and other signs left by otters in two lakeland areas in southern Sweden. The fact that many of the signs such as dens, faecal deposits and runways were visited regularly and by generation after generation indicated territoriality in action, but what really clinched it was finding that the

29

traditional faecal spots in one otter's territory had a repellent effect on other otters—mostly of the same sex. Scent from the anal glands is the carrier of this keep-off message cum ID card. It is squirted in small quantities over the droppings as they are deposited and tells visiting otters the sex and status of the owner, its age and how long ago it passed that way. These identity labels have the advantage of remaining viable for several days and allow a population of dispersed individuals to keep tabs on one another. Sometimes blobs of scent alone are deposited on top of a mound of soil or a tuft of grass which has been twisted into greater prominence by the otters themselves. According to studies carried out at the Institute of Terrestrial Ecology in Aberdeenshire, the message here probably has more to do with breeding condition than with territoriality (see Chapter 5).

The landowners must keep renewing their 'keep-off' signs of dung and scent by regular patrolling, as not to do so would mean invasion by a neighbour and forfeiture of the territory. Twenty or more spraints can be produced by a single adult in one night. Otter droppings are about 1-1.5cm wide and anything from 2-8cm long.

Patrolling a runway

They are loosely constructed because of the large quantities of fish bones, scales, vertebrae and bits of crab carapaces they contain, and possess a distinctive musky odour. Spraints are usually deposited in prominent places such as the tops of boulders, tussocks of twisted grass, on scratched-up soil, and on molehills, sandbars and ledges under bridges. Marking is concentrated along commonly used highways where otters frequently pass one another, as around the confluences of rivers and by the inlets and outlets of lakes. Erlinge found that marking (with scat or spraint) was often preceded by scratching, especially at these populous bottlenecks and in zones of territorial overlap.

The purpose of territorial marking is anti-confrontation; it is simply a non-aggressive means of stating your position in society. Fighting is expensive and wasteful, costing lives and inflicting unnecessary wounds, and marking obviates the need for nasty incidents. When an area becomes crowded with otters, as Erlinge found in spring and autumn, territory holders step up their vigilance and renew spots they left unvisited over the winter and summer. One spring, he counted 35 regularly used spraint heaps along 800 metres of a stream that formed the outflow from a lake. Transients and neighbouring territory holders avoid certain stretches of boundary completely during these seasons of hectic stake-claiming, and use other stretches only when the resident otter is not in the vicinity. Although face-to-face conflict has never been witnessed in the wild by any zoologist, it must occasionally happen and the two opponents probably enact a series of threat signals —raised body postures and loud snarls, which captive bitches with cubs have been seen to use in retaliation to male 'interference'. Fighting itself has never been observed even in captivity and it is most likely very rare; threat signals are invariably successful at forcing a trespasser to retreat.

Except when courting and mating, dog otters and bitches with cubs go their separate ways, the males remaining within their own bit of real estate, the family group keeping to theirs. Because the European otter does not form cohesive groups it is described as solitary, which in the dictionary of a sociobiologist is the opposite of social. There is no such sexual independence of territory in the Asian clawless otter, *Amblonyx cinerea*, and nor is there any in the giant otter, a species I have studied in the wilds of Guyana for many months. In these very social species, the close-knit family groups of mother, father and young share and defend a common territory.

Sam Erlinge found that in inland habitats dog-otter territories come in many different sizes. The dimensions depend on the topography of the area, the status of the landowner in relation to his neighbour's position in society and the 'personality' of the male himself. Family group territories, on the other hand, are all of similar size. Erlinge observed in the Swedish lakes and streams he studied many examples of the presence of neighbouring dog otters placing a constraint on territory size. A dog otter with a territory that included Lakes Säbysjön and Söljen extended its range to the river Svartan (the outlet river from the two lakes) after the dog otter previously occupying the latter stretch had disappeared. Male otters low in the hierarchy, young adults that have just reached maturity and are looking for a territory of their own, are left with the real-estate dross, the rejects of the higher-status otters. Their territories are invariably small and of inferior quality, stuck out in back-of-beyond areas where there is less likelihood of picking up an eligible virgin female.

'Higher-class' dog otters own and defend territories two or three times as large as those of the 'working-class' males. In favourable otter habitat, as much as 12 miles (19km) of stream or 3-6 square miles (5-9 sq km) of lake are defended by one adult male. The average for a bitch and her one to three cubs is about 6 miles (9km) of stream and 1-2 sq m (1.5-3 sq km) of lake, though her territorial borders grow and contract according to season. These figures apply to optimal habitats where food, holt and privacy requirements are more than amply satisfied. Erlinge found that many Swedish lakes constituted good otter country and contained a high density of animals, as many as 1 otter per 2km of shoreline or 1 otter per 5km of stream. Undisturbed coastal habitats are even better, according to a study carried out by Kruuk and Hewson along Scotland's north-west coast. They estimated 1 otter for every 1km of marine shoreline, though the real length is probably more than 1km because they did not take into account the irregularities of the coast. Average territory size is actually larger in second-rate habitats such as fast trout streams and lowland rivers subjected to human disturbance, because a greater area

Portrait of adult male otter, Ben (*Beverley Trowbridge*)

Cubs playing in the grass, their coats wet (*Beverley Trowbridge*)

Portrait of an adult female (*Ron Eastman/Wildlife Picture Agency*)

Back scratching! (*Bridget Wheeler/Otter Trust*)

is needed to provide the same benefits. As a direct result, otter densities are much lower, as little as half that of prime localities.

It may seem strange at first sight that a family group of up to four otters should possess a territory much smaller than that occupied by a single dog otter, but mother otter has sense. She is more concerned with the quality of her home than with its size and chooses an area that is rich in food. Her careful judgement ensures that both she and her cubs will be well fed even in winter when times are hard. Male otters are less concerned with a stable food supply than with sex, and the large size of their territories has much to do with the way in which bitch territories are positioned. In all the inland habitats so far studied, the territory of a family group lies *within* the territory of a dog otter but it is so arranged that a small slice of it spills over into the neighbouring dog otter's enclave. This means that every male has within his boundaries at least two family groups, giving him access to at least two adult females. The bigger a male's property, the more females are likely to set up home within it, an arrangement which, by all the tenets of modern socio-biological theory, is a good thing because it gives him a better chance of sowing his seed more widely. His genes are therefore more likely to survive into the next generation long after he himself is dead and gone.

In contrast to the dog-otter arrangement, boundary overlap is not on for family groups. At no time of the year do they share any part of their area. The closest their boundaries ever get is in autumn when food is scarce and the females are compelled to enlarge their homesteads to the point of overlap. In summer, when family-group territories are at their smallest because there is food a-plenty, a neutral buffer zone exists between adjacent territories; the end result is that family groups seldom if ever come into contact with one another, the frenzied defence of property being left largely to the adult males. Tulloch, however, puts a spoke in the wheel by saying that he has seen different adult bitches using the same coastal holt on separate occasions. Also, in two Aberdeenshire lochs, Jenkins has observed two family groups occurring together and occasionally combining into one group. Suffice to say that, because of otter individuality, there is always room for the exception.

Otter ranges in coastal habitats appear to be different from those

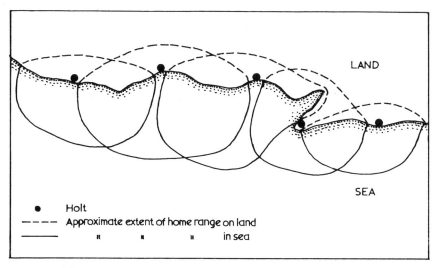

LAND

SEA

- Holt
- - - - Approximate extent of home range on land
———— " " " in sea

9 Coastal home ranges, showing more extensive overlap at sea than on land. Based on Kruuk and Hewson's 1978 sightings off Scotland's Ardnish peninsula

occupying freshwater streams and lakes. From Kruuk and Hewson's study of otter movements along the Ardnish coastline of north-west Scotland there emerged a completely different picture of home range, degree of overlap and sprainting activity. As mentioned earlier, these same scientists found that otter ranges in marine habitats were small, about 1km of coastline on either side of the main holt. Dr Kruuk told me they were unable to relate the movements to territory because of the difficulty in identifying individuals from direct sightings. And for the same reasons, males could not be distinguished from females. Using footprints as an identification aid as Erlinge did on the sand and soft mud of his study site was impossible here, as the ground did not lend itself to well-defined imprints. So we do not know whether the bitch's estate is located within the male's as occurs in inland habitats, or whether each sex has its own mutually exclusive territory. None of the ranges appeared to extend for any distance inland and this means a high population density confined to the coast. The most surprising finding, however, is the total absence of any sprainting heaps around the borders of the 'territories', indicating a substantial overlap between adjacent properties. The boundaries are so fluid they are non-existent. The only sacrosanct areas are the holts, located among the rocks and caves of the shore. A large spraint heap at the entrance of each otter's holt firmly spelt out where tolerance ended and defence began.

Such a peculiar spacing-out system among marine-dwelling otters is interesting in view of what other carnivore species do when their density increases. The spotted hyaena, *Crocuta crocuta*, and the European badger, *Meles meles*, for example, define their territories ever more precisely when conditions become cramped, and tend to concentrate scent-marking activities around the boundaries rather than anywhere else. Kruuk and Hewson suggested at first that the coastal otters' extensive overlap of ranges may have been a response to a superabundance of food. But this idea was later squashed when it was seen how hard the otters worked when hunting—finding food was not all that easy. Perhaps, then, in a habitat where trespassing is easy via the sea, defence is most effective close to the holt. Clearly, to try to defend a territory which is open on all sides would not only be exhausting and time-consuming but also strategically difficult. The holt is an easily guarded stronghold, as access can only be gained by blatantly ignoring the keep-out warnings written in the spraint heap. The theory is unproven and Kruuk and Hewson are still searching for the answer.

A population of European otters is not made up solely of territory-holding adult males and family groups. As in so many animal species labelled territorial, there are also individuals with no home base. These homeless rovers, as much as one-third of any otter population, include low-status adolescent males and females who have just reached sexual maturity at the age of two to three years, and one-year-old cubs who have recently gained independence from their mothers. In many other animal societies, this nomadic clan also contains old males and females who have lost their territories to younger individuals and who are really just waiting to die. Strangely enough, however, there have been no reports of depossessed oldsters in populations of the European otter, which implies that territory holders may defend their home ranges until they die. Summer and winter are the seasons when the 'temporary residents', as Erlinge called the loners, are permitted visas to enter and stay within defended properties; in autumn and spring, when otter activity increases, the landowning dog otters and family

37

groups make their power felt. The visas expire and the temporary residents are expelled into the poorer food areas, becoming 'transients', otters on the run.

The tension and effort involved in maintaining a territory must be extremely expensive in terms of energy expended and stress suffered, both for the intruder and the defender. Exactly what benefits, then, do otters derive from territoriality? It acts as a sort of behavioural contraceptive; it keeps the population density on an even keel by spacing out individuals and by inducing their dispersal. The agents of dispersal are the unmated loners—the transients and the temporary residents. Preventing an otter metropolis from forming ensures that the inhabitants of a given area do not over-exploit their food reserves, a turn of events that would almost certainly guarantee disaster for the population. The dispersion which stems from territoriality also reduces the likelihood of inbreeding, which could lead to congenital abnormalities of one kind or another and limit genetic variation. Without genetic variation natural selection would fail to operate and the species would become an evolutionary dead-end, collapsing into extinction.

Goodness knows how many more animal species would be extinct by now had it not been for modern management techniques and a hard-headed quantitative approach. Today's conservationists must needs be a mathematical breed—they cannot avoid arithmetic. Gone are the good old subjective days of simply watching an animal and writing down what it did. Sums are all-important now and can no more be ignored by a modern ecologist than Einstein could have refused to learn his multiplication tables. The truth of the matter is that quantifying observations is useful because not only is subjectivity minimised but a lot more information is gained. If, in a population of otters, we calculate the ratio of males to females and the proportion of young (animals less than two years old) as opposed to the proportion of sub-adults (two to three years old) and adults, we can tell by applying various formulae whether the population is stable, increasing in numbers or declining. Monitoring the population structure, as it is called, is particularly important if the area has to be artificially managed. Wardens of parks or nature reserves must know if they should cull some of the animals, how many and on which age group

Finishing off a rabbit

and sex they should concentrate. On the other hand, if the population is declining, they may have to take immediate remedial steps. The objective, mathematical approach has proved invaluable in regulating populations of elephants, warthogs and wildebeeste in many of the famous wildlife parks of East Africa.

With conservation in mind, Erlinge calculated the population structure of otters in a south Swedish locality for eight consecutive winters. He estimated that 25-38 per cent of the otters living there were young animals, 30-40 per cent were sub-adult temporary residents and a similar 30-40 per cent were landowning adults. By making counts every year, he discovered that the proportion of one age group to another remained roughly the same, meaning that otter numbers had neither increased nor decreased over the eight-year period. In some parts of the common otter's range, population

39

structure changes with season. For instance, in Sweden there are more births in spring than in other seasons and this creates a small but noticeable explosion of young animals in early summer. As a result, dispersion also tends to be something of an annual affair in this part of the world. Compared with its smaller mustelid cousins, the common otter contains a rather modest proportion of young whatever the time of year. This is a natural consequence of small litters, annual or bi-annual pregnancies, a long pre-pubertal (2-3 years) period and a long life expectancy (10-15 years). Mink, on the other hand, have five to six young in a litter and more than one pregnancy per year, take a mere year to reach sexual maturity and have a life expectancy of as little as four years. The proportion of young in some mink populations is consequently almost twice the figure for the otter.

Whatever their age-group status, all individuals of an otter population must take their place in the social system. Aside from dispersal and population control, a territorial way of life affects both daily and seasonal movements, one effect being that transients have to keep moving during spring and autumn but can stay as temporary guests of territory holders over the summer and winter. No account of a creature as far-ranging as the European otter would be complete without a description of its patterns of travel.

3
An Otter's Travelogue

Otters are very shy animals seldom active during the day. They leave their holts to go fishing as dusk begins to fall and make sure to return before the dawn ripens into day. Raising otters in your house is a good, if sleepless, way to check up on their routine and Philip Wayre noted a peak of activity between dusk and midnight and another around dawn.

Many people believe the European otter used to be a creature of the day and that human disturbance and persecution gradually forced it into a nocturnal mode of life. In the more deserted lochs of Scotland's west coast, there are otter populations that go about during the day and other otter sightings are made from time to time in secluded river systems further south. For example, a correspondent to the *Daily Telegraph* (25 September 1980) said he saw a wild otter one day while out fishing on the River Swale near Healaugh in Yorkshire. And I was recently told by a local farmer of an otter hunting one cloudless afternoon by the waterfall at Kirkby Lonsdale in County Westmorland. So, though we lack hard evidence, it may be that diurnal otter populations were once the norm rather than the exception they are today. Such activity inversion was certainly experienced by the wild cat, *Felis sylvestris*, which has suffered so much from human disturbance that it now seldom hunts during the day. Wildcats share the otter's shy sensitivity in being particularly vulnerable to invasions of their privacy. If the European otter did undergo a change of habit from day to night activity, then it seems that an internal clock has been bred into them, because captive-born otters are still much more active at night than during the day.

The common otter does not migrate like the Aleutian populations of the sea otter, but nevertheless it travels large distances in a short time. Some of the old naturalists had the impression that the movements were either random—a kind of every-which-where activity—or that they simply followed fish-spawning aggregations. They were mistaken. The otter has regular travelling patterns and although the day-to-day timetable is variable, the major seasonal phases are fairly easy to predict.

Dog otters cover much greater distances than family groups because they have a considerably larger territory to patrol. On a winter's night, 5.5-6 miles (9-10km) is nothing to a territory-holding male compared with a more modest 1.5-2.5 miles (3-4km) for a bitch and her cubs. The arrival of spring has little effect on the distances dog otters pursue but cues the family groups to extend their nightly journeys by another kilometre or so. A female otter must always ensure that she and her cubs are well fed and so as soon as the winter ice melts she swim further afield in search of good fishing areas. At the same time, she expands her territory to its maximum limits and spring (as well as autumn) is the season when the boundaries of adjacent family groups become contiguous. In Sweden, Erlinge found that during the rutting peak in early spring, female transients sometimes travel for long distances in company with transient dogs. One such pair managed 6.8 miles (11km) in a single night.

For landowning otters, these sort of distances mean that every night they cover roughly a third or a quarter of the shore or stream comprising their property. An otter should therefore cover the whole of its range in three or four nights and make a regular return to the 'starting point'. But in reality the schedule rarely conforms to such clockwork routine. Dog otters actually cover their territories unequally because they prefer to spend most of their time in the central core. This does not mean there is no pattern to their movements. For example, in spring and autumn when otter activity is high in Sweden, a dog otter whose territory extended along the whole length of the River Svartan and included about half of Lake Säbysjön would frequent the upper part of the river, the preferred core, for four or five nights running and would visit the remainder of the territory on the subsequent two nights. Each territory holder has his own personal itinerary, so that individuals may spend, say, ten consecutive nights in their central core and three nights in the peripheral parts. Excursions to the borders of

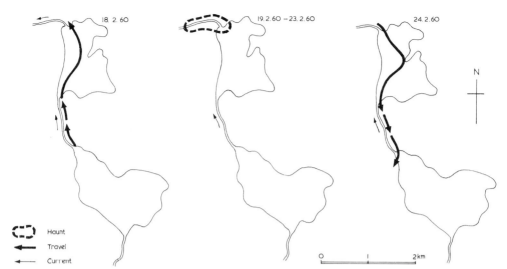

⊂‑⊃	Haunt
←	Travel
←	Current

10 Haunt and travels of a family group in Sweden's Lakes Ellestadssjön and Snogeholmssjön, showing a continuous week of activity, 18–24 February 1960 (*After S. Erlinge*)

the homestead are important to all male territory holders. They cannot afford to ignore their scent-marking responsibilities in those outlying runways frequented by other otters. The inflows and outflows of lakes are particularly busy bottlenecks where transients converge as they enter or leave the lake. But there is something else that will force a dog otter from the cosy surrounds of his core, and that is the presence of a female in heat. So stimulating is a bitch in this condition that a male will temporarily neglect his defence duties. Family groups, in their turn, alter their pattern of travel according to the occurrence of favourable feeding haunts. These change over the year and are not necessarily situated in the centre of the territory. In his studies of the otter in north Holland, Veen estimated there were favourite feeding spots every two miles or so.

Otter activity shifts gear with the seasons. In spring, watercourses that froze over and were abandoned in winter are reoccupied. Otters become very active and travel long distances to springclean their old rolling places and dens and to renew their traditional spraint heaps. Summer is an idyllic time for the otter. Movements decline sharply and activity is confined to a few favourite places, some family groups taking this to the extreme and spending all summer in one place. Even dog otters are not as mobile, and although they continue to patrol every corner of their ranges, the forays are less frequent; trips made inside the core area are short and irregular. Scent signalling continues but at a much lower level and only along the 'public highways' are spraint posts maintained. An otter's summer has an aura of easy contentment about it; as temperatures rise comfortably and the aquatic larder abounds with food.

The pulse quickens again towards the end of August. Movements and scent marking increase and home ranges are more evenly exploited for food as summer-abandoned spots are revisited. Temporary residents are forcefully encouraged to remove themselves from their host's territory and don the nomadic cloak. They realise the 'get out' messages must now be taken seriously and respond by becoming transients, moving away from the area and taking pains to avoid any other big boys whose territories they have to pass through. It is not really known why landowners become more possessive of their territories in spring and autumn. In autumn this 'showing-of-the muscles' may be a physiological response to temperature and day length which 'predicts' the limitation of food in the coming winter. Springtime aggression in bitches may be because there tend to be more births around this time and the females want their territories to themselves to ensure both food supply and privacy. But it is more difficult to understand the reasons for springtime intolerance by territory-holding dog otters; it is true the pattern of food availability changes at this time of year but there are no food shortages. Perhaps the answer lies in studying aggression cycles in the more tropical populations of the European otter, in places such as northern India and the Mediterranean where the climate is more uniform.

Where the winters are cold enough to freeze the lakes, the otter is forced into streams and the inflows and outflows of lakes which fortunately remain ice-free and good for fishing. As in summer, life is once again fairly sedentary, but this time it is not so much voluntary laziness as inactivity enforced by the vicissitudes of weather. Suitable winter haunts are hard to find and otters have been known to travel up to 20km over a two-day period in search of them. In localities such as the coasts of western Britain, France and Scandinavia, otters are known to leave their freshwater haunts and make for estuaries and the sea, as these rarely freeze over. It has even been suggested that salt water helps to rid otters of ticks. A Master of Otterhounds in Devon and Cornwall used to vouch for this by claiming that the otters his pack caught near the coast were exceptionally free from ticks. Predictably, the population becomes clumped in winter and as many as eight individuals have been found crowded into a 2.5-3 mile (4-5km) length of stream. These are mostly temporary residents that over-winter in the unfrozen parts of a landowner's territory. Densities this high never occur at other times of year, even in summer, and the situation requires mutual forbearance. Outdoor activity and spells of intense cold are as incompatible to otters as they are to humans but they do not hibernate. Instead in periods of bitter weather they dig down under the snow and wait it out in their subterranean igloos, leaving not so much as a whisker to be seen. Bouts of mild weather or hunger will entice the furred eskimos back into the open and can sometimes lead to a change of winter quarters.

When an otter visits a part of its territory it does not just swim around and eat fish but stops off at a number of strategic places. These are landmarks that have been modified in one way or another by the otter to fulfil certain needs; many of them are conspicuous to human observers, providing important signposts of otter activity. There are dens (holts), rolling places, couches, slides, feeding places, runways, sign heaps and spraint ing spots, and most of them are near the edge of the water. Dens are found scattered around every otter's home range, except in marine habitats where they are concentrated close to the sea shore. Dog otters have them as well as bitches, so they are not used solely for breeding. They also serve as daytime lodging places and as temporary beds for a quick post-midnight nap. Some of the dens are used more or less permanently, whereas others are only temporary shelters; these may be hasty constructions under a snowdrift or inside a pile of brushwood. For permanent resting places the otters make secluded refuges up to 30 feet (10m) underground, taking advantage of old rabbit burrows, natural cavities among bankside rocks and the roots of ash, oak and sycamore trees. Breeding dens are a definitive feature of a family group's home range. Their architecture is not very different from that of dens used solely as resting places (a full

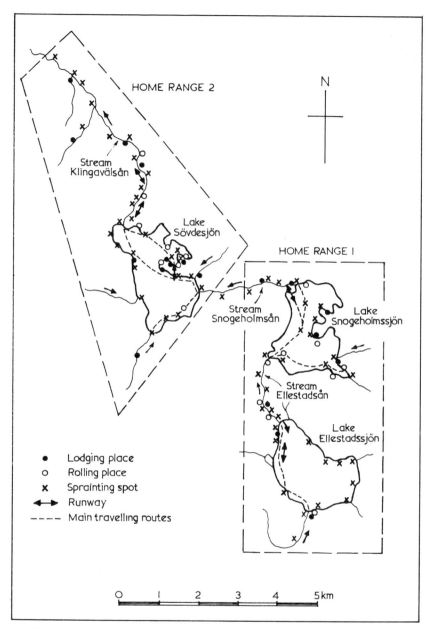

11 Home ranges of two family groups, with the most frequented lodging places, rolling places, sprainting spots, runways and routes (*After S. Erlinge*)

description is given in Chapter 5 on breeding).

Every territory has eight to twelve rolling places where the otter dries and grooms its fur after leaving the water. To find a rolling place you would have to search carefully under willow or alder bushes in the most undisturbed parts of the otter's range and look for an access path leading up from the water's edge. A rolling place is no more than a patch of earth about one square metre in area where the vegetation has been rubbed away and the ground smoothed and compacted. Grass and soil make a very absorbent towel and a wet otter takes full advantage of this, writhing from side to side in snake-like fashion, belly prostrate and chin furrowing the substrate. Fresh molehills are particularly handy for getting dry as the fine particles make a most efficient mop and help remove the stubbornest of eel slimes. Rolling places are more commonly seen in coastal habitats than in lowland stream areas where the grass is lush and does the wiping with little modification. They are also larger and more frequently used in family-group home ranges and it seems likely the cubs treat them as open-air playgrounds.

Some ecologists hold that the excavated towelling cubicles may also function as 'musking places' and that otters deposit scent at the same time as they dry themselves. It was the behaviourist Wynne-Edwards who used the term 'musking place' to describe a high-smelling otter site on the shores of a small loch in the Isle of Lewis. And the Swedish scientist Sam Erlinge also asserts that otters not only dry and groom themselves on rolling places but go on to 'roll on their backs, whirl round and deposit scent material', though it is not clear whether he actually observed this behaviour or whether it is reasoned presumption on his part. The increase in the number of rolling places during the spring and autumn when territorial marking is stepped up speaks in favour of the musking theory.

Rolling places can also double as couches. These are traditional resting places which otters build on the banks of a stream, lake or island and occasionally in secluded locations further inland. A well-worn trail leading to the water marks the spot. Hewson made an extensive study of otter couches at Loch Park in Banffshire. The construction is simple and the materials used are more or less what is around: rhododendrons, panicled sedge and dried fern in some places, stems of willowherb and meadowsweet in others. Dead wood scraped from decaying logs is also used when available. Most of the couches at Loch Park were oval, about 3ft by 2½ft (1m by 75cm), some about half that size. The plant material is pulled off and loosely gathered together, stems parallel, to make a raised platform; as this is laid on in the middle it becomes hollowed to a depth of 2ft or more. Couches are invariably located on flat ground in contrast to slides, yet further examples of otter handiwork, which are worn areas on a slope.

Few authors write about the European otter without a mention of their slides. These, the most headlined of otter signposts, are essentially pathways that otters can slither along, and while the vast majority slope down a river or lake bank into the water, others are made on level ground on snow or ice. There are many stories, some undoubtedly true, of otters playing 'slideys' for hours on end, repeatedly climbing up a bank and whizzing down again and again with every indication of great enjoyment. Both Erlinge and Wayre counter these tales by saying that although otters do seem to use slides as an incidentally playful way of moving, tobogganing games are probably the exception rather than the rule. Wayre himself recalls one such occasion when on an island in a Scottish sea loch. He found a 3-4ft (1m) high slide on a steep sodden peat bank. 'A trickle of water ran from a marshy area up on the hillside, down the slide and into a small pool filled with sedge and rushes. In the middle of the pool there was a large rock on a mound and abundant evidence that the otters had been running round and round the rock, up the bank where the slope was shallow and back down the slide into the pool. The tracks were worn smooth and when I found the place they were still wet with recent use.'

Otters are creatures of habit and have a network of fixed runways to prove it. Many other mammals have a similar system of pathways and crossroads, especially fellow members of the mustelid family: the badger, for example. A diagram of an otter's route system makes Spaghetti Junction look like a road-planner's dream. A great many of the runways are visible as trodden pathways on mud or snow, but some of them are like invisible shipping routes, running across lake and river. The runways on land interconnect with those on the water, forming a cohesive road pattern that is used for generation after generation. The traditionalism of runways is seen in the way otters will continue to travel along old overgrown river beds long after the water has been diverted into more convenient channels for man's use. In some districts of Norfolk where streams were deflected in the twelfth and thirteenth centuries to feed the old corn mills, otters still traverse the runways of their ancestors in the original riverbeds. They do this even though there are deep canals nearby which have been around for more than 500 years. Unfortunately, there are times when an inflexible custom is fatal. Busy roads that are built across runways become otter graveyards. An otter's territory may be cut in two and in trying to take its traditional route from one feeding area to the next the unlucky animal faces likely death from a speeding car. Paul Chanin recorded five otter deaths in the space of six years in precisely the same spot, indicating a mortality level that must exert a drain on any population.

To reduce these road casualties, the Otter Trust is consulting the Norfolk highway authority about building underpasses in vulnerable areas. They are simply 1ft (300mm) diameter concrete pipes just above the water level and to one side. One has already been constructed near the mouth of the River Glaven just outside Cley on the north Norfolk coast, where the river runs under the road, and several others are planned.

The otter's water routes generally follow the shoreline, except where short cuts are taken across part of a lake or river. On land, the runways lead up to dens, rolling places, couches and sprainting spots, or they may form a bypass over a finger of land between two lakes and across loops of meandering river. Overland detours are sometimes made to avoid obstacles such as rapids and fishing nets. As J. Veen observed, 'It seems more likely that the otter covers more distances walking and not swimming', and there is no doubt otters will travel many miles on all fours to get to some distant holt or to cross from one stream to another. Marie Stephens, in her 1957 report on the otter in Britain, mentioned otters being flushed in the daytime on the Montgomeryshire hills, and a Scottish landowner claims to have seen them travelling over hills above the 1,500ft contour. Otters also used to be frequently caught in traps set in rabbit holes far from rivers and are occasionally bolted by ferrets.

It is remarkable how otters manage to keep the same highways in harsh winters, when snow obliterates just about every important landmark and ice forms on the water surface. A frozen aquatic runway deters the otter not one bit; what cannot be swum through is walked on. Temperate Tarkas must either have an amazing facility to memorize the layout of their territory or they must rely totally on reading the scented signposts through layers of snow. It is probably a bit of both, but certainly wherever there is food to be had the resourceful otter will find a way of getting at it.

Upright tripod posture, using hind legs and tail to balance—all the better to see and hear

The broad, whiskery male features in close-up (*Bridget Wheeler/Otter Trust*)

Holt made in peat on the west coast of Scotland, with spraints visible on nearby moss (*Beverley Trowbridge*)

4

Fishing for a Living

Heaven for an otter is a slow-flowing lowland river rich in coarse fish, with a healthy fringe population of birds, mammals, frogs and crabs. Equally favoured is a nice long stretch of deserted shore, which provides a well-stocked marine larder on one side and on the other a fine selection of rocky crevices in which to build a home. Anything else is less than perfect. Fast-flowing trout rivers, which probably contain more boulders than edible aquatic life, make a second-rate otter habitat, though this is what some low-status otters have to make do with. In the last hundred years, pollution and the tremendous growth of towns, cities and roads have robbed otters of a great deal of prime habitat in Britain and Europe. Heaven is receding into the past.

Though we know that the otter is a carnivore, its diet consisting largely of fish whatever habitat it may choose or be forced to live in, we do not know for certain how often otters eat in the wild, how much they eat at a sitting or how much they require every day. Given that the vast majority of European otter populations are nocturnal, it would require a singularly dedicated scientist to carry out such a study; and he might not be able to see and follow the beast. Once again, captive otter studies come into their own. They have shown that appetite varies with season (temperature), breeding condition, the size of the otter and the type of food eaten, but that adult otters consume about 20 per cent of their body weight every day, that is, a ration of some 4 or 5lb (2-2.5kg). Presumably, wild otters need rather more because of their greater energy expenditure.

An otter on the hunt is a marvellous sight in the pale light of dawn. He rises from his couch among the reeds and slips into the water with scarcely a splash, his supple, streamlined body gliding through the liquid in a comet of soft ripples. He may travel two or three miles

A

B

12 (A) Silent, shallow dive used for surreptitious escapes and in surface swimming (B) Noisy, deep dive used when fishing or when suddenly surprised. The head points down, the body follows through and the tail hits the water with a splash

before he decides to get down to business and fish. To do this he must dive: he dips his snout into the water as he arches his back into a hump, his hind legs kicking powerfully to provide the downward propulsion. 'The action is porpoise-like,' says Philip Wayre, 'and gives the impression of great power, the body almost doubling up at the start of the dive. Seen from below, the otter plummets straight down, air-bubbles streaming from its coat.' The bubbles come from air trapped in the body fur being forced out by the pressure of the water. Slow exhalation also creates a stream of bubbles from the corners of the mouth and these curl upward and unite with those originating from the coat. To an observer on the surface, a train of bubbles is seen to rise about 6ft (2m) behind the swimming otter.

Even for those of us who can dive well from a starting point on the surface of the water, there is no denying that a great effort is needed to get us down. But an otter dive is something else. The action is so smooth and graceful the animal seems to slide downwards as if it had no buoyancy to overcome. If sufficiently motivated, otters will dive to considerable depths and there have been instances of otters drowning in crab pots set 60ft underwater and in fishermen's bow nets on the bottom of rivers and lakes all over Europe. Otters have lungs of large air capacity and the potential to hold their breath for several minutes but they seldom do so for more than thirty seconds. An anonymous account in *The Field* in 1884 tells how a trapped otter drowned in three and a half minutes and this figure agrees with Seton's estimate of the longest breath being three to four minutes. On the other hand, Gavin Maxwell timed one of his pet otters for a record six minutes. Clearly, it must depend on the circumstances—whether the otter is in a state of excitement or not—and also on how big a breath the otter inhales before diving.

When an otter dives it experiences bradycardia, a sharp, twentyfold decrease in the pulse rate which produces a sudden slowing of the blood circulation. Bradycardia is a respiratory adaptation of aquatic and semi-aquatic mammals. It ensures that oxygen in the bloodstream is not used up too quickly and so allows an otter, whale or porpoise to hold its breath underwater for much longer than any terrestrial mammal. This is a real advantage for an animal that has to travel and feed itself by diving and swimming underwater. The purpose of a dive is to attack the fish quarry from below, as fish can see only what is going on above them. An otter that has spotted a suitable prey will suddenly move faster and pursue it from below, keeping to a distance of about one metre. Thirty seconds or so of this and the otter comes up for a quick breather, only to resume the chase again. He twists and turns effortlessly using almost imperceptible flicks of his rudder and webbed feet and it is only a matter of minutes before he performs the *coup de grâce*. The fish is seized around the gills in a flurry of bubbles and frantic wriggles. The element of surprise in a low-angle attack is useful because it allows the otter to economise on time and energy. Even so, for every fish caught there are probably several that have managed to escape through speed or tactics. An otter will quickly recognise a fast or crafty fish as a bad investment and redirect his efforts towards more profitable targets. Some fish, like the slow-moving eels, roach, bream and gudgeon, fondly believe they can escape among the weed and stones, but by hiding they actually make it easier for the otter to corner them.

Otters sometimes perform the impossible and bag two fish at a time, either carrying both between the jaws or one in the mouth and the other tucked under one foreleg. Food is never stored, and having made his catch the otter swims to the bankside and tucks in immediately with all thirty-six teeth, holding his prey down on the ground with his forepaws and tearing away mouthfuls of flesh. There seems to be no preference for starting with tail or head, though this may not be true for all otter species; Nicole Duplaix observed giant otters to tackle most of their catches from the head.

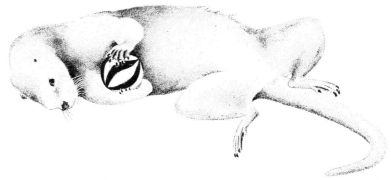

13   Although not as dextrous as the Asian otter, the European otter uses its fingers to grip fish and play objects

Neal vouches that 'The habit of eating prey in a particular spot is widespread in otters,' but there is little evidence to support this claim for any otter species. My own observations on the giant otter in Guyana showed that this species eats wherever it happens to catch its fish. This is usually in the shallows by the forested creek banks, and while bits and pieces may drop from their mouths (things like crab and crayfish pincers, carapaces and claws), they do not consume their meals at any specific spots. Otters are, after all, opportunists and to have to travel to pre-positioned 'snack bars' before eating would be a singular waste of energy. The hearth-sized heaps of fish scales, bones and other solid remains on giant-otter marking sites are not food crumbs but the remains of numerous spraints that have disintegrated and been tamped down by the pair-bonded male and female. There is nothing to suggest that traditional dining-tables are a regular hallmark of the European otter either. Small piles of the pharyngeal teeth and scales of large cyprinids have occasionally been identified as the work of the otter, as have the half-eaten remains of particularly large fish and birds, but never any traditional eating areas. Coastal caves often contain a shelf of rock on which piles of fish bones and crab offal have collected but they could as easily be old latrine heaps as food remnants.

An otter will even occasionally consume his meal in the middle of the river or lake, treading water with his hind legs so that the fore-paws are left free to grip the slippery fish. The clawless otters of Africa and Asia use their almost webless fingers with much greater dexterity. Holding a crab in one hand, they will pluck off the appendages with the other, much as you would the segments of an orange. The morsel is then spooned into the waiting mouth with the finesse of an upper-crust dowager at a Buckingham Palace tea party. The European otter has no need for such delicate table manners. All prey items are pinioned to the ground or held between the forepaws before being passed onto the molars. These tubercled back teeth clamp and crush simultaneously, the prey being chewed six or seven times on one side of the mouth then shifted to the other side to be given the same treatment; as already noted, the otter's gullet is narrow. Small bones such as vertebrae and fin rays are mostly swallowed whole but to be on the safe side, the otter protects itself against potential spears by producing a quarter of an inch thick coat of mucus on the gut walls. It is to this intestinal mucus that otter spraint owes its sticky mucilaginous texture. The mucous shield is important because digestion in the otter is rapid (one to three hours depending on the type of food) despite the long 11ft (3.3m) intestine that characterises aquatic carnivores. Consequently, large bits of bones (and in the case of one giant otter spraint I inspected, a glove-sized piece of fish skin) often come out in the scat unchanged. Sometimes, though, the mucous cylinder fails to do its job and the intestinal epithelium gets scratched. Blood-covered droppings are a sign of this failure; a male otter belonging to a Miss Pitt had a habit of producing them. This particular individual never seemed to realise that otters should chew their food properly and insisted on bolting his meals like a domestic dog. Another pet otter belonging to a Captain Joynson in Wales started leaving blood-smeared droppings and it turned out that the poor creature had developed an abscess at the back of his tongue as a

57

Otter in snow inspecting . . . and eating a freshly killed rabbit (*Beverley Trowbridge*)

result of a puncture from a splintered rabbit bone. The animal suffered great pain and loss of weight but recovered rapidly once the abscess had been lanced. Marie Stephens came upon spraints covered in blood during her 1957 survey of wild otters in Britain, so it appears that intestinal injuries are not exclusive to captive specimens.

Food prospects are excellent by the sea but even there the resident otters still have to work hard at procuring a meal. When Kruuk and Hewson observed otters off the Ardnish coast of west Scotland, they found they swam as many as 760yd (700m) from holt to foraging ground. The feeding area itself was no bigger than Wembley's football pitch, about 5,900sq yd (5,000sq m), and searching for a meal took as much as two hours—much longer than in a lowland stream habitat—each dive lasting about half a minute. The two scientists did not suggest why fishing in the sea was such toil but perhaps it is because many of the fish species are faster and have no bank sides to hinder their escape. Some meals come more easily: Kruuk and Hewson noticed that at certain times of day when the tide was coming in, hunting was carried out in the shallows beneath the kelp fronds where fish are abundant and easily caught and eaten.

The otters Kruuk and Hewson observed on the remote shore of Scotland's west coast are some of the very few European otters which are active during the day. They can hunt by sight, but how do the great majority of European otters, the ones that hunt at night, find their prey? Can they see in the dark well enough to catch fish? There used to be an unspoken belief that all otters, whatever their choice of working hours, caught their fish by sight rather than by smell, sound or touch. As both ears and nose are shut off under water, it is reasonable to assume they play little part, if any, in hunting. That leaves the otter's sense of touch. J. Green has shown that the dense growth of whiskers on the snout comes into operation when the water is murky and vision obscured, but it must also do so on moonless nights. It would have to be proved that otter eyes are either especially sensitive to infra-red rays (given off from all living creatures) or capable of acting as image-intensifiers before we could brush aside the perception of touch as being of no account under normal conditions. A dark night must make vision difficult underwater—whether the water is clear or silted is then irrelevant.

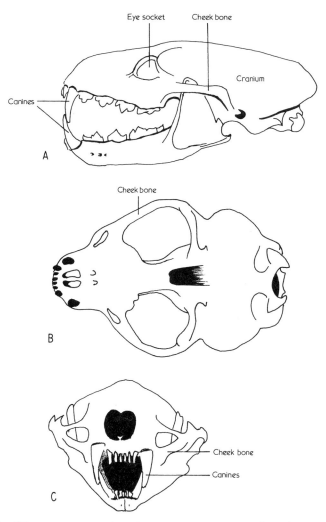

14 Skull of European otter: (A) side view; (B) upper jaw from below, showing tooth sockets; (C) front view

A simple experiment carried out with a captive otter in the dark in clear water would resolve the uncertainty and it is surprising no one has yet attempted it. First, the animal would be blindfolded and its success rate at catching fish recorded. The procedure would then be repeated without the blindfold, and then again with no blindfold but with the vibrissae cut (otter whiskers grow quickly so the animal would not be without them for long). If, when blindfolded and still bewhiskered the otter is as successful as when it can both see and feel, and when de-whiskered and able to see it frequently misses its target, then we could conclude that sight is not all that important for the nocturnal European otter on its regular nightly hunts.

One thing we do know for certain is that otters are born with some ability to hunt. The technique is polished up by trial and error as the animal gets bigger and more coordinated, but the basics are wired in from the beginning. Sam Erlinge watched a six-month old otter cub set out to hunt living prey for the first time in its life. 'It gave chase very eagerly, splashing in the water and making fumbling catching attempts. It did not retain the fishes it caught and its first crayfish pinched its whiskers. However, the otter soon learnt (with no help from its mother) to hunt and handle its prey more efficiently.' Philip Wayre also describes how he took two hand-reared, four-month-old otter cubs to a river and swam with them in his wet suit. One female cub confidently caught and ate a stickleback in the first half-hour though she had never before been in water containing live prey. Once past the preliminary failures, a young otter is no more gauche than an adult twice the size. It searches the water systematically and the luckless prey earmarked for capture is tracked with controlled movements, the climatic snatch being made after a short, rapid chase. But however accomplished young otters may be at the whole thing, they betray that special sense of fun which is the hallmark of all young animals, humans included. Little otters create more splash and commotion than their adult peers, engaging in playful games of 'ball' with the fish they capture, tossing the lifeless creature into the water and retrieving it before it reaches the bottom of the river. No way does an otter cub feel that a full belly is any reason to stop chasing prey. It continues its pursuits with unabated enthusiasm though it does not then eat the fish it catches. Rather wasteful, you may think, but play-fishing is nature's way of reinforcing an inherited skill, a kind of practical, do-it-yourself course to complete the theory she provided in the womb. Adult otters, on the other hand, expend only what energy is needed to assuage their hunger. This is not to say they have entirely lost their sense of fun and play: the capers of adult pet otters clearly demonstrate that they retain a sometimes irrepressible joie de vivre.

While fishing may be fun for some, it is not a cooperative affair in the European otter, at any age. Every individual seeks his own meal, apart from the first five weeks after weaning when the bitch will bring back fish to her cubs. Once this period is over, mother and young fend for themselves. They hunt together as a family but the cubs are now independent as far as catering is concerned and catch their own fish. One of Philip Wayre's otter cubs, Cockle, once dared try to share his mother's meal but was received with such hostile snarls that he was left in no doubt as to his parent's feelings on self-sufficiency. Even the sea otter and the giant otter of South America, which both form social groups, do not pack hunt co-operatively, as wolves do. The only otter species to form cooperative fishing teams is the social Indian otter, *Lutra lutra nair*. This species goes around in groups of up to ten, which when hunting, will form a large semicircle and drive fish into the shallows where they are easily pounced upon and consumed. Occasionally two of Erlinge's captive European otters happened to chase the same prey but there was never any cooperation, and indeed one otter sometimes reacted aggressively if the other joined his hunt. However, work by two American scientists, Sheldon and Toll, showed that the North American otter is not quite so opposed to cooperative hunting on a small scale. They observed a female and her

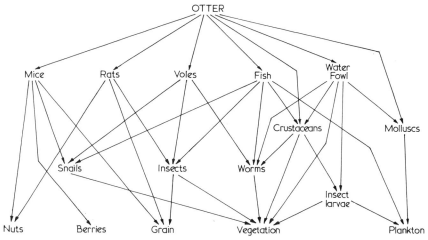

15 The otter's food chain—he fears no predator except man

cub hunt together in a true partnership. With rapid movements, they would coax fish into a shallow cove and then ambush them in the makeshift corral. The results were highly successful, which was more than could be said when they went solo. On their own, they hunted in deeper water and swam on the surface in a leisurely way, head lightly submerged to see what looked promising down below. If a likely victim was spotted, they would make a quick dive and reappear after a few moments, most likely empty-mouthed.

But up to a point otters can afford to take as long as they like to find a meal. They are in the happy situation of having nothing to fear in the way of regular predators, man apart. Like the lion, the jaguar and ourselves, the otter is a carnivore at the apex of a food web, the boss of its own animal-eat-animal chain. In India and Africa, the odd crocodile, leopard or tiger may take the occasional otter if the opportunity arises, but they do not actively seek out otters as part of their daily routine. With no predators to worry about and no rivals competing for food, the otter used to live an idyllic existence. Then man gradually made his presence felt. The otter was branded a pest and accused of large-scale thieving of man's property: lambs were killed, poultry runs raided and fish stocks devastated—all by the one and only arch-criminal, the otter. Spot a group of unsuccessful anglers wringing their hands at the side of a stream, or a couple of farmers poking at the wounds of a dead sheep, and ten to one they would be calling the otter every name under the sun and blaming him for their predicament. The accused was prosecuted and in the absence of a defence, condemned to death by shotgun, dogs and traps. The effect these early exterminations had on otter populations in Britain and Europe is assessed in Chapter 9. Here we review the accusations in order to see what food people thought the otter desired and ate as a matter of course.

While not innocent of every misdemeanour, the otter was often accused on the slenderest of evidence and, in some cases, on nothing more than hearsay. Partly to blame were the naturalists of the day, who chronicled the accounts without trying to temper the bias. In 1869, Gurney tells how 'During a hard winter many years since, a large male otter attacked and killed a sheep in a field at a considerable distance from any stream, at Briston, in Norfolk; and a man who brought some turnips to the flock, found the otter regaling itself on its victim, and killed it with the tail-board of the tumbril. . . .' Sherlock Holmes would have been horrified to hear a conviction on such filigree evidence. The man had not actually seen the otter attack the sheep, it may have been already dead and a hungry otter may have simply taken advantage of an easy meal—otters do occasionally eat carrion. Strangely enough, Gurney republished the account twelve years later, with the addition that if he remembered correctly the sheep had been killed by a bite in the neck. With this belated postscript, Gurney lost any credibility he may have had, but unfortunately the harbingers of otter doom did not stop there. Other equally circumstantial evidence was put forward by J. W. Harvey as recently as 1953 to support the belief that otters killed lambs:

> During the recent lambing season 44 lambs were destroyed in the space of three days. . . . All the carcasses bore tooth marks in the back of the neck, and all had been mutilated by having the heart and liver torn out, these latter having been eaten. The same thing has occurred during three previous lambing seasons, although on a smaller scale. The attacks were attributed to otters, and in fact, ceased abruptly when a pair of otters were hunted and killed.

It would have been as reasonable at the time to claim that foxes or mink—or dogs—were to blame. Moreover, the hunt for the alleged culprits could quite easily have put the wind up these other likely suspects, which would explain the sudden cessation of the murders.

There were a few attempts to put things into perspective. Lancum wrote in 1951 that in the fifty years he had been a naturalist he knew for certain of only one instance of an otter killing a lamb and went on to say that not one farmer in a thousand would ever have cause to complain about the otter. A few doughty correspondents of *The Field* in their turn upset the anti-otter fishing lobby by declaring that removing otters from a trout stream actually did more harm than good. In streams of the North Riding of Yorkshire, where the otter had been rooted out, the number of eels and coarse fish increased, to the detriment of the coveted trout population. The explanation lies in the fact that eels and coarse fish, the otter's favourite food, regard trout and salmon spawn as a child regards ice cream, eating the tiny eggs before they have a chance to develop. In the state of Illinois, USA, in the late 1930s, the introduction of predators like the otter was actually recommended and experiments on Lake Windermere also led to an abrupt change of policy after they showed that the fish population benefitted from a reduction in their numbers.

That otters are not partial to trout and salmon and had nothing to do with an angler's disappointment in his weekend fishing was confirmed by food studies made in Sweden, America and Britain. Depending on the habitat and the time of year, the otter's diet was found to consist of 70-90 per cent fish with a wide variety of small mammals, frogs, water fowl and crustaceans making up the rest. The non-fish part of the menu may seem insignificant but it is an important side dish as it means the otter is not totally reliant on fish. Not all otter species consume such a large fish portion. The diet of the African clawless otter, *Aonyx capensis*, for example, is chiefly crabs and fresh water snails; fish are caught only in the dry season when they are trapped in small pools. *Aonyx* lives in the vash marshes of tropical Africa and is far more terrestrial than aquatic being, as one naturalist put it, an otter 'bent on returning to land habits'. At the other end of the scale is the totally aquatic sea otter which inhabits North America's Pacific coast and the seas around the Bering Straits. The sea otter, ironically enough, does not eat fish and it is starfish, clams and giant abalones—those sea-egg goliaths—that form the bulk of its diet. The full-time seaman is a specialist feeder and has even evolved a very advanced and sophisticated form of tool use, wielding a stone to crack open the hard outer skeletons of its prey.

Not so the common otter, which flaunts its true carnivore colours in acting the opportunist. It takes whatever is easiest to catch and this usually means whatever is most abundant at the time, whatever is slowest and whatever is small enough to kill easily. Eels satisfy these provisos nicely and to an otter, an eel in the pond is worth two trout on the run. Wherever eels occur in abundance, they form a substantial part of the otter's daily bread. They are every inch a good meal and even ill otters with poor appetites cannot resist them. It is claimed that otters living in marshes near the sea are particularly fat because of the abundance of eels there. Wayre used eels to entice his recalcitrant cubs back into their enclosures at night after their customary post-prandial

Eating an eel on the river bank (*Angela Potter*)

walk. It was a simple case of using the carrot ploy: 'Dangle an eel, chant "eels, eels, eels", and they would follow you to the gates of hell,' says Wayre. And there is one otter on record that did just that. The eel it had swallowed stuck halfway down its throat and choked the poor otter to death. Perhaps it was too big; otters usually go for the 20 to 30 inch (50-75cm) specimens.

Coarse fish are snapped up almost as frequently as eels and include roach, perch, pike, bream, rudd, tench and burbot. Fairley and Wilson's study in Ireland showed that fast sportsfish such as trout and salmon, which were locally abundant, made up less than 14 per cent by weight of the otter's food intake; those that were taken were mostly handicapped by old age, disease or fin wounds. In a captive set-up, Erlinge discovered that otters go for medium-sized coarse fish around 4-6in (10-15cm) long, the very young and the very large individuals being rejected because they were either too fast or too difficult to handle. Otters that make a living by the sea go for crabs and for bottom-dwelling fish such as butterfish, pollack, flounder and lumpsucker.

As the waters of stream and lake warm up with the approach of spring, the cold-blooded fish prey are galvanised into action and some species become difficult to catch. So the otter turns its attention to sedentary creatures, which multiply around this time of year. Frogs and crustaceans are nuzzled out from under stones and young waterfowl are snatched by swift attacks on unguarded nests. Frogs are especially plentiful in spring when they form large mating groups and in autumn when they again amass for hibernation. As winter approaches, fish lose their zap and once again figure prominently in the otter's diet. At this time of year, eels bury themselves in the mud and are easily prised out and caught. Even when a lake is iced up, otters will continue to hunt and Hewson observed one noisily making elliptical holes in the ice on Loch Park in north-east Scotland.

Otters catch adult water birds by the same tactics as they normally use to catch fish. They sneak up on the duck, coot or whatever feathered victim is lined up in their sights, by swimming underwater and striking from below. The bird is seldom quick enough. Frogs, on the other hand, are treated differently and with something approaching sadism. Wayre has seen many of his otters prepare a frog for the chop and he always ends up feeling sorry for the luckless amphibian. The otter first of all indulges himself in a little appetiser entertainment by forcing the frog to jump repeatedly and then when boredom sets in the exhausted high-jumper is held down and chewed slowly. By observing many of these grisly scenes from beginning to end, Wayre squashed the popular belief that otters leave frog skins turned inside out. These morbid remnants are left by rats which also treat toads in the same way. With toads, Miss Pitt's pet otter used to substitute thorough washing for the *hors d'oeuvre* entertainment of forced jumping but this habit probably had a function—to get rid of excess acid secretions from the skin.

Analyses of otter spraints and stomach contents show that they also ingest bits of grass, leaves, stones, earth, wood, straw, their own fur, insects and earthworms. Most of these are probably incidental garnishes to the main meal of small mammal, fish or frog: the insect remains for instance, are probably derived from insects swallowed by

67

the fish which the otter ate, but there is no doubt that some of the plant material is taken in deliberately. Otters have been seen to eat the bark of aquatic trees and Gunn was informed on two or three occasions that in times of hardship otters will eat thistle roots and dig up vegetables, eating both roots and the leaves. There is also the odd tale of pet otters becoming a nuisance by helping themselves in their owners' vegetable patches. This is unfortunate because they are good slug-removers and if trained properly might become a gardener's friend! Perhaps they consume plant food only when animal prey is scarce, but this is very likely an over-simplification; they probably get important vitamins from certain plants and might, like sick dogs, seek out grass and other green material for its medicinal properties.

It is in captivity that otters' eclectic tastes become truly evident. You can be certain they will dispatch a wide range of goodies, from the leftovers of Sunday's bean stew to grandma's failed Yorkshire puddings. I once gave a captive giant otter a digestive biscuit, a piece of coconut and some rain-soaked bread, and so delighted was she with the assorted flavours that I was assailed with a barrage of 'wau-wau-wau's' when I attempted to call a halt to the meal. European otters are just as greedy and have been known to consume birthday cake, mashed potato, cheese, porridge and, by mistake, even headache tablets. This easy-to-please attitude to food extends into other aspects of otter life—breeding-season preference, for one.

5
The Single-Parent Family

The European otter is not fussy about when it should breed. Young cubs have been seen with their mothers at all times of year and captive births have also been recorded in virtually every month. The otter births at London Zoo took place on both occasions in August (1846 and 1856, respectively), while Cocks' female produced her young in October (1881) and eight litters belonging to Wayre entered the world in several different months. In *The Otter Report* of 1957, Stephens recorded 134 occasions on which cubs were seen in the wild in Britain. From an estimation of their size and weight, it was possible to calculate roughly the months in which each litter was born, and the investigation showed that births occurred throughout the year. The inaccuracy of the method is obvious, as the age/weight figures were only approximations, but as Stephens pointed out the error would be equally distributed throughout the year. In Scotland, north-west France, Sweden, Denmark and Germany, the common otter is known to breed whatever the season, but there do tend to be more winter and early spring matings here, since male-female pairs are most often seen travelling together at this time of year.

The North American otter does not go along with year-round fertility and generally mates in spring, giving birth some nine to twelve months later. The reason for such a long gestation is delayed implantation, a suspension of the embryo's development so that birth is timed to coincide with favourable spring conditions. Some other mustelids, such as badger and mink, also experience this restraint in egg development. The important point here, however, is the seasonality of the American otter's mating activity; our native otter's continuous willingness was not realised by naturalists in the past. On the contrary, assertions that it has an identifiable breeding season could fill a dozen chapters, but these were either pure guesswork, often embellished from someone else's suppositions, or based upon the flimsiest of information. Cockrum stated that winter was the otter's breeding season, Bell and Erxleben selected 'March or April', Novikov 'April or May' and Daniel 'about the month of June'. Lloyd was a little vaguer, declaring that dog otters 'feel the need for feminine companionship' once or twice a year.

The confusion over whether the European otter mated and bred all year round was initially cleared up by wild sightings and captive observations of young cubs, but a recent study has provided evidence of a different kind. Gorman, Jenkins and Harper of Aberdeen University found that their captive female came into heat every thirty to forty days throughout the year and not just in winter. Each period of oestrous lasted about two weeks, during which time the female produced numerous blobs of jelly-like scent, her nipples enlarged, her vulva became swollen and discharged fluid, urination increased and she became receptive to the advances of the courting male otter. Her behaviour changed from guarded vigilance to an inviting display of rolling on her back and making moaning noises. In the wild, male and female otters lead separate lives until they are ready to mate; but, asked Gorman and his colleagues, which one is the first to be ready? It used to be thought that the female came into condition first and let her suitor know she was available by laying a trail of perfumed messages, depositing the scent produced by her anal glands on the spraint heaps around the perimeter of her territory, and leaving small quantities to be carried on the currents when swimming. The message to the patrolling male is 'I am female X and I am available'. The Scottish scientists did not dispute that scent was the communication system deployed to indicate readiness to mate but they did kill the notion of the female's leading role.

According to their study, the dog otter himself produces blobs of jelly-like anal-gland secretion and, like the bitch, does so intermittently. In fact, the onset of the captive male's deposits was precisely synchronised with that of the female's, which implies the male comes into breeding condition only for two weeks at a time. The Aberdeen scientists went on to discover that *either* sex could initiate the two-week bout of scent deposition and that the physiological onset of oestrous did not automatically trigger the production of scent in the female. Sometimes the male beat her to it, and his scenting activity then immediately triggered her own. The big question is how, in these instances of dog before bitch, the male knows when his partner is set for oestrous so that he can pre-empt her and be the first to turn on the scent. The female must send out some sort of signal, but just what it is has yet to be found out.

Stephens was told a rather different story by a long-gone generation of hunters during her study of the otter in 1954-56. According to these oldsters, the male makes preliminary contact with a female by 'love whistling', which was reckoned to be quite distinct from the whistle used when hunting. Moreover, if two dogs favoured the same bitch, fierce fighting ensued with the opponents first challenging each other vocally from a distance. French naturalist, Joseph Levitre and others claimed to have witnessed the next and bloody stage of these passion fights, when the aim of each dog was supposedly to attack his rival's penis. One of Stephens' informants said he actually saw one dog castrate his rival, though if this is true it must be a most wasteful and agonising way of saying who's boss. Certainly there are some nasty fights in nature but nowhere else in the animal world is the end-product of a fight a eunuch!

However the two sexes are brought together, it is now up to the male to carry the budding relationship a stage further. Much of what happens next has never been observed in the wild and our knowledge is based on observations of various captive otters belonging to London Zoo, A. H. Cocks and Philip Wayre. The dog makes several attempts to approach the female but she does not always respond as he would wish and often plays out a hard-to-get pantomime, chittering irritably if he gets too close, and on occasions lashing out at him with her forelegs in a more physical display of antipathy. But this paragon of suitors, the dog otter, is nothing if not patient and presses home his advances with a persistence that makes Eros look timorous. Wayre observed how, at this stage of the affair, his captive bitch happened to be lying on her back in the grass when the male 'rushed in and rolled against her on his side but jumped up and right over her before she could bite him. While doing this he moved his rudder very vigorously from side to side in a pronounced scything action.' Wayre feels the tail-wagging was a defence strategy, as he has seen Indian smooth-coated otters and Asian short-clawed otters do the same thing while they were eating in order to ward off another approaching from behind. The whole otter courtship scene is more like something out of a judo contest than the lead-up to a love scene.

As oestrous sets in, the bitch begins to respond to her hormonal upsurge by rolling round frenetically on the grass, sometimes on her belly though more often on her back, front paws waving in the air. Then things really start to happen. The two otters begin to chase each other in the water in much the same way as a dog plays with his owner, running madly at him only to sheer away at the last minute, a sort of watered-down predator-prey chase. Mating may take place now or a few days later, depending on the individual otters. Every otter has a distinct personality and some male-female pairs prefer to get to know each other better before mating so that a bond of affection develops, albeit an extremely transitory one. Wayre found it was no use forcing a relationship that had not taken off naturally and at least one of his male-female pairs failed to work up the necessary twinkle-in-the-eye and so never mated. The courtship phase is brief and, during it, successfully betrothed couples sleep, eat and play together, a far cry from the tense relationship of the previous stage.

Copulation is prefaced by vigorous bursts of play chases and mock fights, as if the act itself were not energetic enough! The dog pursues his hard-earned mate in and out of the water, the two diving and corkscrewing through the cool depths together. Tiring of this, the pair pretend to fight each other as, with only their heads above water, they lunge forward at face and neck. The bitch eventually lies still on the surface with her back awash and her rudder arched just clear of the water. The dog quickly mounts from behind, grasps her loins between his forepaws and her neck in his jaws, then bends the lower part of his body around and below the base of his partner's tail, alternating short bursts of pelvic thrusts with longer periods of rest. Copulation in Wayre's European otters lasts between fifteen and thirty minutes, and during it the pairs would repeatedly roll over sideways and often disappear below the surface of the water. The successful mating of Cocks' otters in 1881 lasted almost three times as long, 'the female loudly chattering or whistling in a peculiar way all the while'. Liers'

North American females also vocalised loudly during copulation, but the sound was an altogether more raucous caterwauling. Additional matings may take place over a period of several days, depending on how long the pair keep together.

Much the same sequence of events must occur in the wild, barring perhaps the early stages when the male first comes into contact with the female and offers her his attentions. Outside the confines of an artificial enclosure, in the open space of her natural habitat, the bitch probably feels less hounded and more able to escape from the initial advances of the male. The female's irritable behaviour observed around early oestrous may be, to some extent, artificially induced by the inescapable and persistent presence of the male within the enclosure.

In captivity, the male is generally removed from the female as soon as she is seen to be pregnant, which is often as late as a week before birth. If left with her, the male ends up with more than just hurt pride and a black eye; female otters become true bitches after birth and make no bones about wanting to be alone. The heady courtship relationship between otters in captivity is severed in the same instant as the umbilical cord, and the female suffers a prolonged bout of post-natal aggression rather than depression! The dominance roles are reversed and it would be a foolish dog that tried to trespass over a bitch's boundaries during this period. There is the occasional mild-mannered female that does not shun her partner quite so emphatically, but these tend to be in the minority. No one knows exactly what happens in the wild, but sightings of male-female pairs are scarce and it seems that the dog parts company with the female soon after the last mating session, perhaps after no more than a day or two of being together. He may well get onto the scented trails of the other females whose territories lie partly within his own. As no lasting bond is forged with any of the females, he will have no compunction in behaving polygamously and in terms of evolutionary success, the more widely he spreads his sperm the greater the chance his genes will have in surviving to the next generation.

The female confines her investment for genetic immortality to the cubs that are already forming within her womb. She raises her babies with no help from the male. It sounds like another case of sexual discrimination in the animal world, but the male has his own work cut

Pair of otters resting (*Ron Freethy*)

out patrolling his territory and making sure that both transients and neighbours are kept aware of his status. And, after all, he was not given much say in the matter in the first place, being forcefully directed by the female to get lost; it would not be fair to say he deliberately opts out. Countless years of evolution have seen to it that the arrangement is one of mutual consent. Even so, there is evidence for believing that the father keeps an eye on his family; he will sometimes occupy a holt near to the family group's holt and is occasionally seen accompanying them for a few days at a stretch. There is also one heart-warming story of a male otter in California taking on the responsibility of the half-grown offspring he had sired after their mother had died in a trap. For months he shepherded his little ones away from the steel traps concealed along the otter runways and continued to do so until the cubs were fully grown.

This was an unusual case, but it is normal for a male giant otter to be a paragon of fatherhood. Every day he tends his young as assiduously as the female does, and never leaves the family group by itself. What is more, he chooses to live with the same female year after year, and it is therefore not surprising that a deep bond of affection exists between the two of them. So strong is the relationship that if one of the pair is killed the other becomes pitifully distressed and is loath to take on another mate. It remains a bachelor or spinster for the rest of its life, losing much of its territory to other groups, or else it takes on the subordinate role of adolescence and becomes a transient. The emotional disruption of losing its better half is also mirrored in a complete evaporation of aggression, a change of heart that makes it easy for land-grabbing neighbours to take over. The Indian clawless otter has a similar society of close-knit family groups but the sea otter, though living in large groups, is not family-orientated. Males are segregated from females and, just as in the European otter, every mother looks after her own offspring while the fathers remain anonymous by keeping within the precincts of their exclusive club.

Pregnancy in the European otter lasts some nine weeks and in this time the female's nipples enlarge and she puts on weight, particularly if she is going to have more than one cub. There is no delayed implantation as in the North American otter so it is fairly easy to predict roughly when a captive litter should be born. As Wayre's experience has taught him, it is impossible to be accurate to the day, because there is always a chance that a later mating may have gone unseen during the night. A maximum and minimum period can be determined by taking into account the actual length of time the male and female were together. By removing dog otters after different periods, Wayre and his helpers recorded a minimum possible gestation of 61 days and a maximum of 74 days.

Pregnancy is not a time of rest for a bitch otter. Besides having to feed herself well, she must modify at least one, if not more, of her holts so that her cubs will be warm and comfortable. Nesting holts are no different from ordinary holts, most of them being the underground type—converted rabbit burrows linking an entrance at the surface with a resting-chamber below. Some holts, like the temporary one Erlinge found excavated beneath the snow, have a lateral cul-de-sac tunnel which serves as a toilet. Holts in coastal habitats often run right back into the hillside with many entrances and a selection of dry caverns for nurseries. Kruuk and Hewson found a heap of excrement at the entrance of most shoreline holts on the Ardnish coast of Scotland and deduced that these were more than just a front-door loo.

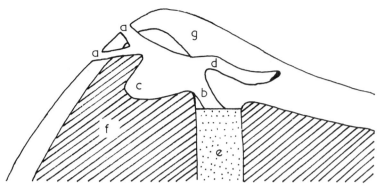

16 Ventral section of an otter holt in a hillock (f), partly made by excavating overlying snow (g). It has two entrances (a) above water level, a main resting chamber (c), a side tunnel (d) ending in a spraint heap, and an escape tunnel (b) leading to a ditch (e)

They served an active territorial function.

In secluded areas safe from human interference, breeding holts may be made in the open, beneath dense stands of brambles or on beds of reeds in marshy regions. Hollow trees, drainage culverts, town drains and even sewers have been known to do just as well. There is an unusual case of a bitch who made her nest under the floorboards of a clergyman's dining room. The otter family was discovered one evening during dinner after the cubs' high-pitched cries prompted the parson to have the flooring lifted.

Such urban holts are exceptional and the norm is for the bitch to select a breeding holt in the remotest part of her territory, often up a small side-stream. In parts of Scotland there are tales of otters travelling miles overland to remote highland lochs for the express purpose of finding a holt to give birth in and raise a family. Whether these travellers were pregnant females seeking a breeding holt is questionable because bitch otters are always reluctant to leave the security of their territory and especially during this crucial period.

Both dog and bitch in the European otter line their dens with a combination of soft and woody vegetation. Grass, reeds, moss, water plants, the odd tuft of sheep's wool and finger-thick twigs are all torn up and transported to the holt by mouth. Twigs are probably not the most comfortable mattress to lie on but they do keep the animal dry by ensuring an efficient circulation of air. In fact, however, some holts cannot possibly be kept dry, especially those with only an underwater entrance where the bedding gets damp from the otter's dripping coat. Philip Wayre noticed that his otters did not go out of their way to select dry vegetation, so it seems that their efforts at constructing an aerated mattress of twigs are virtually cancelled out. The only feature that makes a pregnant female's holt different from a dog otter's is the large quantity of fresh material she brings in when birth is close at hand. She makes a hollow in the centre of the nest and settles herself for the big moment.

Otter birth is such a private affair that it has been witnessed only once, and then not in the European species but in North America's *L. canadensis*. The females in question were captive ones belonging to a Canadian naturalist, Emil Liers. As his account is the only one of any otter species on record, it is worth quoting.

> The process of birth lasts from 3 to 8 hours, depending in part on the number of young. The mothers that I have watched stood on all four feet when bringing forth the cubs. One cub after another would be dropped until the entire litter was produced. . . . The female curls tightly round the cubs in such a way that they are almost completely shut off from the cold air.

Liers never mentioned what the new mums did with the afterbirth but if other mammalian mothers are anything to go by, they probably eat it as their babies take their first lungfuls of air.

Newborn otter cubs are a delight to the eye. They are barely 5in, (12cm) long, including the tail—which is curved tightly round the abdomen as in the foetus—and could fit into an ordinary jam jar without any problem. Their coats are a pale grey, not dark and water-proof like an adult's, and contrast softly with the bright pink of their footpads, ear openings and bewhiskered muzzles. As 2oz blobs of toothless, blind fur, the cubs snuggle easily into their mother's curled-up body. She takes on this shape to protect her babies from the cold while at the same time allowing plenty of elbow room for suckling. Should mild danger threaten, she tighten the curve of her body to hide the little ones from inquisitive eyes. Greater danger in the form of a dog, say, or a hunter, prompts the bitch to transfer her litter to a safer den, an instinctive response which has been observed not only in the wild but also in captivity if more than one holt is provided. She will grip each one in turn by the scruff of the neck and dog-paddle to holt number two. To speed up the transfer, she will sometimes swim several hundred yards underwater without any apparent discomfort to the dangling cub. The mother otter that gave birth at London Zoo in August 1846 was observed by Hunt, the head keeper, to hike her cubs regularly from one breeding box to the next at times when nothing in particular threatened her. Hunt could only conclude there was method in her madness, that she was ensuring that the cubs always had a dry bed.

An otter litter consists of anything between one and six cubs but the commonest number is two or three. The cubs are quite helpless at birth and for five or six weeks afterwards. They find their heads impossibly heavy to lift and their little feet make only the feeblest of movements. Interestingly enough, this is quite unlike the sequence of events in human infancy; babies learn to hold up their heads and look around long before they have gained control of their limbs. Where tails are concerned, otter cubs have no fear of movement and they wag them with happy abandon at feeding time, giving the impression of so many motorised matchsticks. At first they suckle every three or four hours for about ten to fifteen minutes each time, struggling upwards through their mother's fur in search of a teat. Being blind, they have to feel for the milk-giving mounds rather than look for them, twittering hungrily until they find their goal. The tiny forepaws stretch out instinctively and knead the area around the nipples to encourage the flow of milk. Female otters have two pairs of nipples though there have been several reports of shot or captive specimens with three pairs. Blyth and Maxwell each recorded a bitch with, surprisingly, two-and-a-half pairs of nipples, the anterior pair lacking a teat on one side. Bellies full, the bitch turns each of her little ones onto its back and licks the area around the anus to stimulate defaecation. She is not so much bothered about burping her charges as about keeping the holt clean and so she eats their soft faeces as a precaution.

Mother otters take their parental responsibilities seriously and only at night do they spare the time to leave the cubs for a quick meal themselves. When young cubs are not feeding they are sleeping, and this they do lying on their backs with paws folded across distended bellies. Fast asleep, they are unaware of the involuntary jerks of their little bodies but S. Shepheard often watched those of her tame otter cubs and remarked how 'the constant and purposeful twitching of their limbs seems to indicate that the cubs re-enact in their dreams the frolics of their waking hours'.

By the fourteenth day of life, the cubs' milk teeth start to emerge and suckling no doubt becomes more uncomfortable for the bitch. Already their anal glands have started to function and to the human nose the smell of the fluid is even more pronounced than the adult secretion, a distinction Philip Wayre discovered to his cost when he picked up one of his fortnight-old cubs! Eyes open about a month after birth, but the cubs are short-sighted at first and objects more than 10-13ft (3-4m) away cannot be distinguished properly. By this four-week stage, body weights have increased to a healthy 1¾lb (795gm) or so, the male cubs already tending to weigh a few ounces more than their sisters. Crawling with head upraised is now possible but walking remains a hurdle for the future.

As the cubs grow, their faces lose the roundness of babyhood and their fur changes colour slowly to a darker grey and ultimately to the sombre brown tones of adulthood. Feed times are less frequent and gradually tail off to three or four times a day. The seventh week heralds a critical phase in the cubs' development. For the first time they emerge, wobbly-legged, from the holt and experience their first taste of solid food. This is usually an eel or some other handable fish which the bitch catches and drops before them. Stephens was told by a number of fishermen that they have seen the bitch land an eel and bite it into pieces for the cubs. If they remain unenthusiastic, she will chew the pieces herself and shake out the chewed ends for the cubs to have another go. As the switch to solid food takes time and patience, the bitch continues nursing until the fourteenth week.

She no longer eats her offsprings' excrements because weaning has brought about a change in their composition and they are now as firm as an adult's. Instead, mother otter encourages her small charges to do their business outside the holt. She considers house-training a very important part of cub-rearing and, when the occasion demands, will handle remiss children firmly. Harris describes an incident involving one of his North American females and her seven-week-old litter of two. One morning, she appeared at the doorway of her nestbox and unceremoniously tossed out one of the cubs, hauling it back in again after a few minutes. The procedure was repeated with the other cub, the bitch appearing to regard the whole thing as routine a chore as putting washing on a line is to a housewife. But Harris was puzzled and could only look on in helpless wonder as the head of his otter household continued to cub-dump over the next few days. It finally dawned on Harris that the bitch was in fact giving her cubs a somewhat unorthodox course in the niceties of house training: because after the rigorous programme, he never again saw them defaecate inside the nest box.

One thing mother otters cannot do is teach their cubs to walk. They must learn the formula themselves, by the time-honoured method of trial and error. Watching a seven-week-old otter cub trying to run creates the same expectant tension in the observer as watching a baby totter ten paces from sofa to chair. Both infant pioneers achieve their target distance but not without collapse seeming imminent at every step. The little otter's coordination and balance are as yet disorganised and its thumb-length legs are still weak. This begins to change after the two-month landmark is reached, when the cubs undergo a spurt of growth and development. The permanent teeth emerge between the milk teeth and gives the mouth a crowded appearance. The leg muscles strengthen and begin to operate in harmony with the rest of the body, an advance that gives play a new impetus. There is now much more jousting among themselves, with a commendably patient mother whose whiskers present a tempting toy to clutch and pull at hour after hour, and with just about anything or anyone who cares to oblige. In this phase of heightened activity and growth, the cubs frequently venture to the edge of pool or river and drop their heads into the water almost as if they were vetting the strange new medium for future use. The head-wetting habit is a familiar one to Wayre who has seen many of his otter cubs test the water in this way.

By the end of the third month, the youngsters have acquired their first waterproof coat and are literally ready to take the plunge. Wayre believes that most young otters take their own first tentative steps into the water with no help from mum; his experiences with his captive otters indicate this. But there are equally authentic accounts of mother otter having to entice her offspring to poke more than just their heads underwater. A little push sometimes goes a long way. Harris gives an amusing account of how his North American bitch had to take firm action with her recalcitrant family, perhaps partly because the pool in the enclosure had a series of rough rockwork steps leading into it instead of a ramp which must have made entry rather more difficult.

> The mother went first into the pool and floated with her head against the top step, facing the cubs (five in all) which were gathered on the edge, and calling to them. When they refused the step she caught each one in turn by the scruff of the neck and pulled it into the pool. The cubs proved extremely buoyant, but rather like swimmers in the Dead Sea they seemed unable to keep an even keel, their legs on one side or the other constantly rising above the surface. Once in, they showed no fear or hesitation. Those which could not get out alone the mother grasped by the scruff and lifted.

Not every mother is as quick to come to the rescue, a failure Liers discovered to his dismay one morning during a routine check of his captive otters. He found one of the cubs, a female, abandoned by the side of the pool and a postmortem revealed her eleven-week-old lungs to be full of water, a straight case of death by drowning. The first-time swimmer must have tired of trying to keep afloat and exhaustion set in before the bitch could reach her. Negligence of this sort is exceptional and probably happens only in large litters when the mother's attention is divided between several cubs. Ward was lucky enough to watch a rather more attentive wild bitch encouraging her young to enter the water. Persuasion having failed to lure the little ones in, the mother otter got them to climb onto her back—perhaps ostensibly to play a game of piggyback as they sometimes do—and once they had responded to this subterfuge, she sank beneath the water. The cubs were left floating like two little stamps come unstuck from an envelope until eventually they started to lash out at the water, holding their heads high above the surface. It was clearly an alarming business for the inexperienced but the ploy worked and the young beginners were soon discovering skills they never knew they had. The bitch's strategy of forcing young otters to swim by enticing them onto her back is sometimes put to good use in an entirely different situation. An anonymous account in *The Field* in 1898 tells of a mother otter with two cubs being chased by a dog. The cubs could only swim for short distances at a time and so the bitch would stop every now and then to allow them to climb on to her back. She obviously could not manage to hold both cubs together by the scruff.

There are other descriptions of wild bitches playing an active part in getting their cubs into the water then standing by as lifeguard in case of need. No one has recorded seeing her attempt to do more than that. The cubs teach themselves by trial and error to dive, dog-paddle and swim underwater and, by all accounts, do so remarkably quickly. Wayre believes the motherly helping hand is the exception rather than the rule. All of the fourteen common otter cubs he successfully reared at the Norfolk Wildlife Park and the Otter Trust entered the water without the slightest prompting from their mothers, who kept a protective eye on them but made no attempt to overcome their hesitancy by pushing, tossing or dunking them in. In describing the development of the litter born at London Zoo in 1846 Hunt, the head keeper, corroborates this. He tells how the cubs simply followed their mother into the water, though they waded in like dogs with their heads above the surface instead of diving in as their parent had done. Almost three weeks were to elapse before they were observed to plunge into the water like adults. Some bitch otters actually have to prevent over-eager cubs from making their water debut too soon. One particularly venturesome male belonging to Wayre was fearless of the water and kept running to the edge of the pond to set off on his own, only to be hauled out, dripping, by an irate mother.

A baby otter's first attempt at swimming is reminiscent of a child's first dip in the swimming baths. The movements are not coordinated and are accompanied by more splashing in one spot than forward thrust. Sometimes, too, the lightweight young find it difficult to dive to any depth, but progress—in the otter if not in the human—is rapid, and soon the cubs swim as confidently as water-babies, revelling in the weightless magic of buoyancy. With this achievement behind them, the growing otters automatically start to hunt. They soon learn that the slow, abundant fish give the best returns for the energy expended.

The bitch is not above cheating a little to help the inborn fisherman in each of her protégés to flower. Several anglers told Stephens they had seen a female otter catch and land a small fish and then put the wounded fish back in the water for the cub to have a go. Youngsters that still fail despite the poor fish's handicap are pushed underwater with a firm paw until they come up with the goods. But captive cubs studied by Wayre and Erlinge gave their mums no cause to worry, as they all caught their first fish without so much as a look of encouragement though admittedly, crabs and crayfish tended to be a little troublesome, at times pinching the apprentice fishermen by the nose.

Up to this point, captive otter cubs are tame and amenable to petting and handling by their human keepers but around the age of three months, when they begin to catch their own meals, there is something of a personality change: they become shyer and less cuddlesome as the trusting innocence of childhood is replaced by awareness of potential dangers. It is almost as if inborn forces suddenly awaken within them to remind them of their ancestry—that they are heirs to the otter race and not to *Homo sapiens*. The fact that the character change coincides with learning independent hunting is nature's way of helping wild cubs protect themselves. With the bitch keeping less of an eye on them, it is necessary that they should become more suspicious in nature and trust no one.

It is not that captive fourteen-week-old otters lose the playfulness of infancy, but that the fun and games are now kept amongst themselves rather than with their human owners. Play is an otter's hobby. It takes up whatever time is left over from hunting, grooming and territorial defence, because as C. J. Harris puts it, 'a healthy otter is never found lying about doing nothing'. Play in all young animals is supposed to help construct the mental building blocks of various 'earnest' behaviours needed in adulthood. The reason young otters continue to hunt fish after they are sated is that they must refine and reinforce their hunting technique; similarly, wrestling among siblings teaches them the basics of self-defence and territorial upkeep. But there are some otter games which seem to defy scientific explanation and which appear to be unrelated to territoriality, mate selection or hunting. Otters will somersault, blow bubbles, balance stones on their heads, chase their tails round in circles, grip one hind foot by the mouth and bowl themselves over like self-made balls, and still be ready to show there is more where that came from. New ideas for games gush like oil from an Alaskan pipeline. Young or old, wild or tame, otters are creatures with congenitally happy dispositions.

Associated with play is the desire to explore and this comes in handy when the cubs reach the age of nine to ten months. Family group cohesion begins to weaken around this time and is the first sign of mother-cub separation. The apron strings are finally cut around the cubs' first birthday and neither they nor their mother look back once the deed is done. At the same time as the female abjures her maternal responsibilities she begins to respond to the advances of the resident dog and starts the reproductive cycle revolving again. The cubs are now on their own but remain in their mother's territory for another few months, though it must be said that this stage of otter development is still hedged about in speculation. By staying in an area where every nook and cranny is known, the young otters gain confidence to travel further afield in search of a territory of their own. Finding a territory is important, because without a home base neither dog nor bitch will breed; but it is an occupation as stressful to an adolescent otter as house-hunting is to a young human couple. Familiar landmarks are perforce left behind and the otters must range through strange country as ignominious transients. Males tend to search further afield than their sisters though both probably take about the same time to stake a claim. If things go well, after six to twelve months of nomadic existence and temporary residence in the territories of high-status land-owners, they will find themselves in a suitable untenanted area. Some will have fallen by the wayside, victims of hunters, fish traps or cars, but the rest will be in a position to propagate themselves. At two to three years of age, the youngsters will have at last become landowners and can afford to relax a little before they go on the hunt for a mate.

At the water's edge—the grace of otter movement (*Bridget Wheeler/Otter Trust*)

A pair of otters at play, male on the left (*Ron Eastman/Wildlife Picture Agency*)

Otter swimming, with eyes, ears and nose above water (*Ron Eastman/Wildlife Picture Agency*)

Female otter with two large cubs, on the Shetland coast (*Bobby Tulloch*)

6
Communication

Social animals do not have a monopoly on communication. For solitary species, information exchange is just as important to integrate the members of a population and to space them out. A territorial society like the common otter's requires reliable news bulletins on who is doing what where. Sight, smell, touch and hearing are the four senses an otter uses to communicate with other members of the population and with the environment, though not all are used to the same degree. Hearing and smell are the most important in terms of the amount and complexity of information conveyed.

Anyone who has kept a common otter will know that it has an acute sense of hearing, sensitive not only to frequencies discerned by human ears but possibly to higher ones as well. Philip Wayre frequently observed his tame otters prick up their ears in response to sounds totally inaudible to him, as if receiving on a different wavelength. And, going back to the 1930s, E. O. Townshend relates an incident with her pet otter which adds weight to this supposition. She was filming her pet which was swimming contentedly in a pond at the bottom of a large disused sandpit. Suddenly something caught the otter's attention and she turned in the opposite direction, rushed out of the pond, ran across the floor of the sandpit and up the steep bank, a distance of some 400yd (360m). She was found on top of the bank avidly consuming a family of fledglings whose nest she had tipped over. It seems likely that she had responded to high-frequency sounds produced by the fledglings. But even if she had only picked up faint chirps within the normal range for humans, the incident still shows that the otter's hearing is more sensitive than our own.

Good hearing in an animal presupposes its ability to produce sounds of its own. It not only picks up noises from the surrounding environment—both animate and inanimate—but also receives auditory information from members of its own species. Social animals have a large number of sounds in their vocabulary, some of them being subtle variations on a theme used to convey equally subtle differences in mood or meaning. Nicole Duplaix found the Asian clawless otter was one of the more vocal social otters, and my own work in Guyana on the giant otter has revealed this very social species to possess at least eight distinguishable sounds and a plethora of intermediate gradations. The European otter, for all its being a more or less solitary species, has at least six different calls, with few variants. Whether there are a few more reserved for underwater communication is anybody's guess; no one has studied the subject, but as the ear flaps close under water, it seems unlikely. Though our otter is silent compared to the social otters, its rather inflexible language does play a vital role in its communication system, the more so because it is a nocturnal animal with secretive habits.

Much has been written about the otter's so-called 'whistle', probably because it is the call most frequently emitted in the wild and also because it carries easily over long distances. In Wayre's opinion, it

Otter calling. Note the webbed feet well-splayed on land

is not a whistle at all but a very high-pitched and piercing squeak. It functions to let your mate, mother or cub know where you are and at the same time invites a reply so that you in turn know where *they* are. Scientists call a vocalisation with this purpose a contact call. The European otter is the only otter species which uses a single-note squeak as a contact call; many of its relatives use two-syllable 'wheeuks' instead. The 'whistle' lasts about one second and is generally repeated at least once. On a calm, windless night, it comes across as a plaintive, flute-like sound with a needling quality that pierces the silence. If two or more otters who wish to remain together lose contact with one another, the same call is uttered during the search that follows and Lee gives a heart-rending account of a mother otter searching for her dead cub after it was killed accidentally by a party of men out ferreting. Despite the activities of the men, the distraught bitch never left the area all day and kept re-entering the burrow and whistling in vain. Cubs which have become separated from their mother squeak as much as the bitch who is doing the searching. Some Cornish fishermen laying their nets in a quiet inlet saw two young otters in the water, captured the little creatures and tied them up in the boat. The cubs' fervent screams were very effective in bringing their mother to the scene, her defence instincts primed for action, but the story has a sad ending, for despite her valiant efforts to climb into the boat and save her young ones, the fishermen eventually killed her. Time and again incidents like these crop up in the literature, the shrill squeaks of an otter in trouble bringing help from another otter nearby.

Otter cubs start emitting the contact call when they are about two months old. Before then they seem unable to manage it, but this hardly matters while they remain safe within their nest. What they do produce during these early weeks of life are bird-like 'chirrupings' of apprehension whenever mum leaves them to feed herself or when they can't find her nipples to suckle. The delicate calls provoke subdued 'huffs' of reassurance from the bitch and a repositioning of her body to make her teats more easily available. As the weeks go by, the cubs' chirrupings gradually turn into louder squeals and finally into the shrill contact call of maturity, so that by the time they are ready to leave the nest and brave the outside world, they can give voice as proficiently as any adult.

A sound that otters make frequently during their working hours is a short explosive exhalation or 'hah'! Gavin Maxwell noticed that his Indian smooth otter used it to express a question: it usually happened in the context of walking into a room and looking around in an is-anyone-there sort of fashion. Used by the common otter, however, it means something rather different; a bitch will 'hah' to make her cubs hide when danger threatens and either of a mated pair will use it to alert the other. The alarm sound is no use if the otters involved are far apart because, unlike the so-called whistle, it does not carry far. It is also a surprise response to the sudden presence of an animal or human observer, for example, or a sound of apprehension while investigating an unfamiliar object. Wayre describes how an otter driven by curiosity will approach the object in question and emit a hearty 'hah!', only to retreat a few paces, then repeat the process again and again until it finally overcomes its fear. Hahing is used in a similar context by several other otter species, namely the clawless African otter, the short-clawed Asian otters, the North American otter and at least one of the South American *Lutra* species, *L. annectans colombians*. I have found that the giant otter produces an identical sound for the same reason and Nicole Duplaix's work in Surinam corroborates my findings.

The day-to-day threat call of the European otter is surprisingly weak-sounding to the human ear: a querulous wishy-washy chittering that ends on a rising note. The noise is rather more intense in the Indian races, 'in whose throats', says Harris, 'it sound like nothing so much as the tantrums of a very angry human baby.' Made in a quieter, deeper tone, the common otter's chitter functions as a warning, dispersing an irritant before the big guns of the all-out threat call are used. Quiet chittering is consequently a low-intensity threat and is frequently used by a bitch when her enthusiastic suitor begins his advances during courtship. Wayre had it directed at himself when he picked up Fury, one of his wild-born cubs: she clearly did not think much of being picked up—rather like an explorative toddler who wants to escape from mum's clutches—and expressed her opinion in a burst of impatient chittering. Wayre was quick to put her down on *terra firma*, knowing full well that an agitated otter will bite if pushed too far. An irate animal attacks with bared teeth and gives vent to a harsh, intimidating snarl.

90

At the other end of the scale are the friendly whickering noises which otters make in greeting one another after a period of separation. It is a quiet, confidential exchange which acknowledges a bond of some sort between the otters. Like little puppies, young otter cubs also keep up a constant querulous whickering when playing together, partly as a sibling interchange and partly to let the bitch know where they are.

Some of the sounds to which otters give voice are accompanied by movements of the head, legs and tail, though there is little change in facial expression. Otters lack the facial musculature and mobility of primates, and have less even than the domestic dog. The no-nonsense attack snarl is the only vocalisation accompanied by a definite change in mien. By the time this stage of aggression is reached, the otter has worked itself into a frenzied passion and the lips are pulled backwards over the teeth in a fearsome grimace, the external ears being laid back against the skull in the manner of an angry or suspicious horse. Fear in the face of attack from the rear is expressed by swinging the rudder sideways like a motorised pendulum. It is most commonly seen when one otter has food and is afraid another otter may attempt to steal it and, to a lesser extent, when a dog otter is engaged in currying the favour of his betrothed. In either case, the scything action doubles as a means of defence as well as an index of the animal's fear. Happier emotions are also given their share of physical expression, though not so much facially as bodily. An otter in playful mood will often roll over on its back and paw the air with forefeet held close together. Along the same theme, otters will touch noses when they whicker hello in a brief moment of physical contact which holds the same meaning as the nose-rubbing custom in Eskimos and cheek-kissing in the west.

The fact that hearing develops more rapidly than sight in young cubs shows just how important this faculty is to the otter. But for all that, sight still has a vital part to play; a sightless otter would find it very difficult to fish and to recognise the dangers and familiar landmarks of its territory. Whiskers may provide a sensitive back-up tool for locating moving prey but it is vision that is relied upon most heavily. It is generally believed, too, that otters see better underwater than on land, where image resolution is not quite so good. The eye accommodates to underwater conditions by the contraction of a sphincter muscle in the iris. This squeezes the anterior part of the lens and gives the eye a bulging appearance which often persists for a short while after the otter has surfaced.

Given an animal as solitary, stealthy and far-ranging as the otter, possessing scent glands and in the habit of depositing its droppings at regular sites day after day, it is no surprise to find that its olfactory sense is as important as hearing in its communication system. Odours applied to solid objects persist and convey messages long after the communicator has left the site. They are an especially useful means of social integration for common otters which seldom meet to exchange visual signals. Vocalisations play their part but they are no use for long-distance communication. Scent enables several otters to exchange information without having to congregate, a facility of immense importance for a creature so far-ranging. Wynne-Edwards observed that scent is so vital for social integration that herbivores will leave telltale trails which give away their whereabouts to their predators and some carnivores in turn sacrifice part of the surprise element in hunting because of their own distinct smells. Scats and urine are the guardians of an otter's territory; they let neighbouring landowners and strangers passing through know that the area is not available and that they had better be cautious. The keep-off signal can also convey by its freshness how long ago the depositor left the area, and having been read the message is replied to in kind by the strange otter. Scent

Dominant sniffs the ground before sprainting, while its partner awaits its turn

produced from the anal glands is also very much part and parcel of the olfactory answerphone system and recent work in Scotland suggests it conveys chiefly breeding information, such as the sex, age and reproductive condition of the animal that placed it there. By the oily brown deposits, a male can tell whether or not a female is available and ready for mating and the extent of male rivalry.

Appraising the four orthodox senses on their own does nothing to convey the remarkable rapport that exists between some otters. In his book *The River People*, Wayre tells how during the long afternoons of summer he would release Kate and Lucy into the upper reaches of the River Stiffkey in Norfolk while he and his wife chaperoned them from the bank, making sure they did not get into too much mischief. Of the inseparable pair of sisters, Lucy was the extrovert, the reckless explorer, whereas Kate was more cautious and nervous. One afternoon as they explored the stream and played hide-and-seek among the bushes, Lucy swam off to investigate the opposite bank, leaving a distraught Kate squeaking hysterically in the shallows. 'Finding she was alone Lucy turned back, ran up to her sister and pushing her nose against Kate's two or three times encouraged her to follow. Kate set off, but once in the water her nerve failed her. Again Lucy turned back to her sister, who, reassured, followed her across the brook.' This rather touching episode illustrates a perception that is somehow more than the sum of the four senses. Similar fine feelings were exchanged between a couple of North American otters belonging to Emil Liers. The two adults were allowed the freedom of Liers' home and one day they decided to explore upstairs, where there would be all manner of knick-knacks to excite the curiosity of any hot-blooded otter. Having finished doing this with every sign of enjoyment, the male found he could not face coming back down the stairs; they scared the life out of him. So he called out to his female companion below, who at once climbed back up and led him down slowly, step by step, 'talking' to him encouragingly all the way. In both cases, the stronger otter showed an understanding awareness of the weaker one's predicament and came to the rescue with a flow of encouragement and concern.

But if we talk of rapport then we must look at the otter's relationship with humans, for it is in this partnership that this most sentient of creatures reveals its true potential for communication.

93

7

The Otter in Captivity

If there was a test which showed which animals were the most stimulating and intelligent to befriend, then the otter would surely do well. The almost invisible silence of wild otters gives the impression of a passive personality, but any otter owner will tell you that human companionship seems to bring out the extrovert in them. Our native otter has more charm and vivacity per square inch than half the dogs and cats in Hyde Park or Hemel Hempstead. For centuries otters have been kept as pets in the house, as exhibits in zoos, as unpaid fishermen and, more recently, in captive breeding programmes. The Asian short-clawed otters are apparently the most easily tamed and form a docile and stable relationship with their owners. Close runners-up are the North American otter, the European otter and the giant otter of South America. Sea otters also tame easily but for some reason there is a high death rate among the captives. The species which even experienced people think twice about domesticating are the smooth-coated Indian otter and the clawless African otter, because they are emotionally unreliable and can sometimes literally bite the hand that feeds them.

Owners, past and present, of European otters are too numerous to mention individually. Latter-day owners have ranged from the humble fisherman of India and Malaysia to the mansion-dwelling gentry of England and Europe. But even though times have changed so that it is mainly zoos and conservationists that own otters today, the underlying fascination they hold for us has remained as strong as ever. The otter is a mammal that has always been high in the popularity pet charts of Europe even though it is not the easiest of animals to keep in captivity and is anything but the cheapest. It emanates an enchantment that goes beyond the endearing cuddliness which all furred creatures seem to possess. Its charm is probably as much a product of its high IQ as of its playfulness, wilful disobedience and insatiable desire to explore, the very qualities that make it difficult to keep otters.

Alfred Cocks and Philip Wayre are notable among those who have successfully cared for and bred otters and experienced the happiness and hazards which such an occupation involves. Each has his own idea of how otters should best be looked after but they agree on the basic constraints and prerequisites of otter keeping. There are a number of important points that must be remembered when planning an otter enclosure. The animal's wandering habits must be catered for in some degree, as must its need for privacy—especially if it is to breed—its sensitivity to any kind of stress and, above all, its need for plenty of dry land to rest, dry, groom and play on. In underlining the critical areas where zoos go wrong in otter maintenance, Nicole Duplaix found that this latter requirement was particularly neglected. An otter must be given as spacious a pen as possible, and it must include a sizeable pool, a healthy chunk of dry land at least four times as large as the area of water and a kennel of some sort where it can feel completely safe and private.

Wayre's breeding enclosures at the Otter Trust in Earsham are 100 × 50ft (30 × 15m) or larger and each contains a pool around 40ft (12m) in diameter and 5ft (1.5m) in depth. The excavated pools

Breeding enclosure at the Otter Trust, Earsham, near Bungay, Suffolk (*Philip Wayre*)

connect with one another and with a natural stream, and consequently there is a constant circulation of fresh water between the enclosures. Where it is impossible to contrive such ideal conditions, self-contained concrete pools will do but they have to be cleaned out and refilled every two or three days to keep infection at bay. Breeding enclosures should have pools with sloping edges in order to give the cubs safe access to the banks when they tire of swimming, otherwise they may drown. Wayre advocates natural vegetation such as sedge, reed or grass for lining the breeding holts rather than hay or straw which his

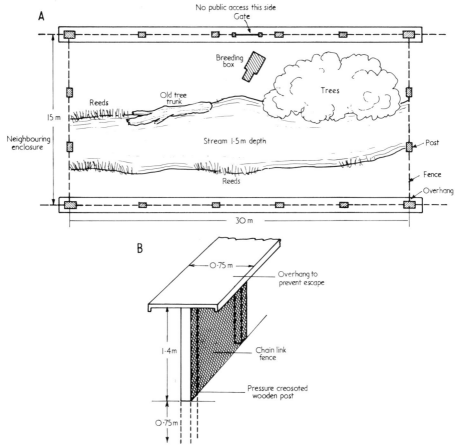

17 An ideal enclosure, at the Otter Trust: (A) plan view (land approximately four times water area); (B) detail of chain-link fence. Minimum measurements given

otters did not like and chucked out as soon as it was put in.

When it comes to toilet habits, otters are fastidiously clean and choose an area within the enclosure to do their business on. With the first ceremonial deposit it becomes the permanent loo and a little fresh sand or sawdust helps to keep the spot dry, odourless and easy to clean. Toys such as branches, hollow logs, tree stumps with dry rot, a waterfall or steady jet of water, stones, slides and sand all help to keep captive otters occupied and are good for their morale, while a cover of bushes, saplings and turf will provide privacy as well as 'lamp-posts' to scent-mark around and groom on.

It all sounds fairly straightforward, making a home for otters and keeping them healthy and happy, but the above pen design and code of practice is the end-product of painstaking trial and error by conservationists such as Philip Wayre and Emil Liers. There are many things that can go wrong through ignorance, lack of facilities or plain bad luck. Food is the biggest problem. Says Nicole Duplaix: 'If misconceptions concerning the otter's aquatic disposition are widespread, those involving its feeding habits are even more tenacious.' You can't just dump a few fish into the enclosure and expect these broad-spectrum carnivores to thrive. And as it is obviously impossible to procure on a daily basis all the different types of fish and other animals an otter would normally eat in the wild, it is important to find a good alternative diet. Many different formulas have been administered with good results and it seems that as long as certain provisos are met, a captive otter will keep in fine condition. Philip Wayre's recipe is:

Fresh minced beef	907g (2lb)
Yeast	14g (½oz)
Heart (ox)	28g (1oz)
Carrot	28g (1oz)

He used to include a few ounces of bran, oats and biscuit meal in the mixture but he told me he stopped this after discovering that one of his otters had developed kidney stones. The source of the trouble was traced to the bran-meal additive, which was found to contain too much calcium for the otter to metabolise properly. From then on it was omitted and the patient soon regained his high spirits and good health. Wayre feeds the above mixture to each of his otters for their main evening meal together with some dead day-old chicks or a few fish, usually whiting, herring or eels. Though expensive, Wayre found that eels are often the only food a sick otter will eat and he also sometimes gives them to new mothers as a reward for the hard work of birth. The only other daily meal Wayre provides for his otters is breakfast, which is a trough-full of fish or dead day-old chicks. Almost all meals in the Wayre otter household are consumed to the last crumb but there is always a poor eater or two to coax and worry over. It is a fact of life in animal-keeping and, for that matter in child-rearing, that some of your charges will eat almost anything on offer but others are finicky and will refuse all but the choicest of items. Adult otters often fit into the latter category, but for cubs every meal is a good meal. At six weeks old they can be weaned on to a fairly high-calorie diet of raw minced beef, finely diced raw fish and the uncooked yolk of an egg. Wayre then gradually substitutes yeast, carrots and ox heart for the yolk and fish, so that by the time the cubs are five months old they are eating the same standard food mix as the adults. Very young orphan cubs have been reared successfully on the popular brands of milk substitute fed to human babies. At this tender pre-weaning age, otter cubs are quite helpless and the human step-parent must remember to perform the post-prandial duties which their real mother would do as a matter of routine. A damp cloth should be used to remove the inevitable dribbles of milk from around the mouth and a wad of warm, wet cottonwool rubbed around the anus induces defaecation as effectively as the bitch's caring licks.

When it comes to the question of how often to feed your otters, there is as much debate as about feeding human babies. Some people feel they should be fed regularly at set times during the day and others reckon you should give a feed whenever they show they are hungry. However, a quick inspection of the various regimes employed over the years reveals that the number of meals is not so important as the quality of the food. Two really good, well-planned feeds a day satisfy the greediest of otters and are convenient for many of the larger establishments with keepers on a nine-to-five work schedule. Once a day is not enough, as Nicole Duplaix discovered in her study of zoo-kept otters in Europe. Duplaix observed that otters fed only one meal a day ended up half-starved and spent hours listlessly pacing around their enclosures calling out for food. A coat in poor condition is often a sign of an insufficient diet or one that lacks some essential nutrient, though it is almost as often due to inadequate grooming facilities. Of course, too much of a good thing can sometimes be as bad as too little, as Wayre's experience with the kidney stones caused by bran-meal taught him. Too many herrings are likewise inadvisable because they cause a deterioration of the coat and, on occasions, even paralysis, being rich in thiaminase, an enzyme which destroys part of the important vitamin B complex. Herring helpings should therefore be given no more than twice a week.

Getting the right nutritional balance is clearly strewn with pitfalls, and the problems of captivity do not end there. Diseases and everyday ailments have to be watched and remedied quickly. Bites, for one, are never in short supply as otters are playful creatures and frequently nip one another while frolicking. Marie Stephens' male otter used to give his female playmate a rough time and although she gave no sign of objecting to the fun and games, she did lose the tip of her tail to him and just missed having one of her eyes speared with a friendly canine. If they are not treated immediately, bites like these are liable to become septic. Broad-spectrum antibiotics keep the germs at bay and can either be administered sub-cutaneously by injection or orally over several days. Dental diseases are similarly non-infectious but they are common because of the otter's peculiar molar make-up. The upper-jaw molars are characteristically too large to fit comfortably into the palate and are therefore prone to impaction and abscesses. Abscesses have to be lanced and drained and followed up with a dose of anti-biotics. Gum diseases also have to be contended with and are commonly caused, as they can be in humans, by a diet of soft foods. This is one of the reasons why fish, chicks and other hard-ingredient items are so important.

Otters exhibited in certain animal establishments succumb easily to chills because of one or more bad points of neglect: dirty water is irregularly changed, conditions are damp and cramped, with the only substrates to groom on being mud and excrement, or the diet is poorly balanced. Chilled otters are prone to the common cold, diarrhoea and, like many other mustelids, feline enteritis. If curative measures are not taken in time, gastro-intestinal complications and pneumonia can develop. Nicole Duplaix found that once the protective mucous layer lining the intestine has sloughed off, enteritis will take a firm hold and death often results within twenty-four hours. The simplest way of keeping these infections in check is to monitor coat condition and scat consistency regularly, as both of these are good indications of an otter's health. A waterlogged coat is one that has lost its water-resistant properties. It is recognisable by the inability of the guard hairs to form normal healthy drainage spikes. Instead, they become matted into a smooth, slicked down overcoat—especially in the sacral region—and the underfur ends up quite wet and sometimes shows through in parts. At this stage of pelt deterioration, otters find difficulty in keeping afloat and will even decline to enter the water. An otter that has lost its capacity to keep dry and insulated is an otter in danger.

Apart from the gastroenteritic bugs, there are other internal parasites that can and do invade an otter's gut, in the wild as well as in captivity. Roundworms, tapeworms, nematodes and trematodes have all been found in otter intestines but none do very much harm if the level of infestation is low. Duplaix reports that otters respond well to antibiotic treatment for these ills but stresses that particular care must be taken to restore the intestinal flora promptly or else there may be serious complications. Mention has also been made of other parasitic infections in various parts of the body. Helminths have been recorded in the cranium of wild otters, and captive otters may also fall victim to leptospirosis (or Weil's disease), a viral infection carried by rats, mice and other rodents which is fatal to the otter and strikes without warning. Canine distemper, although comparatively rare, can also kill if left untreated, while anthrax, hepatitis and blood trypanosomes and microfilaria are also potential killers.

External parasites are as common in otters as they are in domestic animals. Ticks, *Ixodes recrinus* and lice are always found tucked among the hairs of otter pelts. The particular species of biting louse which is found only on the otter in Britain is *Lutrida exilis*. Fungal infections, too, find otter skin a good medium to colonise. Otters confined to damp cement floors often end up with cracked interdigital webbing which if left untreated will make an excellent habitat for *Monilia* fungi.

Scratching the throat

The infection may spread to other sites of the body, such as the tip of the tail, where the fungus is more easily detected as bare, hairless patches. Stephens' bitch otter was once the unlucky recipient of such a persistent tail fungus. Dusting her bedding with mycil powder soon got rid of the invader but it took much longer for her hair to grow back.

The trials and tribulations of maintaining otters in healthy condition pale into insignificance against the enjoyment derived from their enchanting personalities. The otter has won and continues to win the hearts of even the most serious-minded of conservationists. Although Philip Wayre's primary objective is to build up a captive reservoir of the endangered European otter and to study the details of its behaviour, he joins many naturalists and laymen before him in capitulating to the otter's charm. The consequences of allowing otters into the home are often disastrous but nonetheless vastly entertaining. Their overwhelming curiosity makes them quite unsuitable for people who take pride in possessions and frequently leads them into trouble, as Gavin Maxwell explained so feelingly in his book *Ring of Bright Water*.

> Otters are extremely bad at doing nothing. That is to say that they cannot, as a dog does, lie still and awake; they are either asleep or entirely absorbed in play or other activity. . . . There is, I am convinced, something positively provoking about order and tidiness in any form, and the greater the state of confusion that they can create about them the more contented they feel. A room is not properly habitable to them until they have turned everything upside down; cushions must be thrown to the floor from sofas and armchairs, books pulled out of suitcases, wastepaper baskets overturned and rubbish spread as widely as possible, drawers opened and contents shovelled out and scattered. . . . Water must (also) be kept on the move and made to do things; when static it is as wasted and provoking as buried talent.

Maxwell got a hint of these qualities long before any otter actually crossed his threshold. Mijbil was a two-month-old Indian smooth otter, *Lutrogale perspicillata maxwelli*, which the well-known explorer Wilfred Thesiger had bought for Maxwell from a Marsh Arab in Iraq. Maxwell was also in Iraq at the time and faced the daunting task of transporting young Mijbil all the way to England with stopovers in Cairo and Paris. In the few weeks they spent together before the marathon flight, animal and man had become firmly attached to one another but as Maxwell was to discover, a bond of affection is no reason for an otter to abdicate the ties of its nature. The airline authorities had instructed Maxwell to carry his pet as personal handbaggage which meant taking him into the passenger cabin. The plane had no sooner become airborne than a claustrophobic Mijbil escaped

Swimming free in the sea (*Bobby Tulloch*)

After rescue from oil pollution, the cleaning-up process (*Bobby Tulloch*)

Otter with conger eel (*Bobby Tulloch*)

Male otter hiding in seaweed (*Bobby Tulloch*)

from the confines of the small, zinc-lined box, making a panic-stricken beeline down the gangway towards the back of the aircraft. Several shrieks and pacifying smiles later, Mijbil was back on Maxwell's knee, probably more shaken by the experience than any of the passengers on board.

The peaceful slumber that followed was only a temporary respite for an already exhausted owner. Mijbil awoke refreshed and ready to face a new challenge. Target number one was the newspapers which Maxwell had spread around his feet as a temporary loo. Mijbil set upon the printed pages with irrepressed gusto, tearing them into confetti-sized pieces. Tiring of that, he turned his attention to the sawdust in his detested 'coffin' and conscientiously shovelled it out, using his head and shoulders as a spade. To make a clean job of it, he got right in and lay on his back, pedalling furiously with all four feet to eject the stubborn bits. Maxwell was also a flurry of activity, a Charlie Chaplin come to life, as he tried in vain to tidy up the mess his pet was making. The drama took a turn for the worse when, with sinking heart, Maxwell saw the furred tadpole take hold of the adjacent passenger's overnight bag. The closed zipper posed no problem to one as single-minded as the otter; the bag opened up with the sureness of a surgeon's cut and in went Mijbil's head. Out came a miscellany of travelling bric-a-brac: magazines, hankerchiefs, gloves, pills, earplugs, the lot. Maxwell was terrified lest the lady owner would wake up and catch Mijbil *in flagrante delicto* but she remained in deep repose in the seat beside him, quite oblivious of the assault on her privacy. She obligingly got off at the next stop in Cairo none the wiser on an otter's excavating talents or its remorseless appetite for entertainment.

Philip Wayre and his wife have suffered no less with their wayward pets. They would often play host to newly caught young otters, bringing them into their home in order to give them the intense care they needed. In the case of Gutsy and Ripple, not only were they too young to be left outside on their own, they belonged in addition to an Asian race of the European otter (from Bangkok) and had to be gradually acclimatised to the cold of England. The humans were quick in discovering the shortcomings of their home as an otter sanctuary. Otters are wide-ranging creatures adapted for spending half their life in water, and the topography of a house places serious constraints on

105

their activities and tests the endurance of human room-mates. Gutsy and Ripple were the first otter guests to teach Wayre a number of truisms about having an otter as a pet. Despite their cuddly appearance they do not liked to be picked up except when very young, they have a vicious bite which they are not averse to using, intentionally or not, when excited or angry, and their scent glands remain inconveniently active even in conditions as artificial as a brick bungalow. Maxwell's famous Edal was normally a tame and gentle otter but one day she bit her master so seriously that he lost two fingers as a result. Wayre found that as Gutsy and Ripple grew up the relationship between his otters and himself changed subtly. They lost their desire to be in the house and were inclined to bite harder and more frequently. In all fairness to the otters, the more painful bites may not have reflected any sadistic intention on their part; they may have simply reflected the growing strength of adolescence. A playful bite to a tough-skinned otter is a serious wound to a tender-skinned human, and when you are left holding a bloody hand the underlying motivation is largely irrelevant.

But if an otter is sometimes unpredictable he can also be the model of self-restraint when interacting with his human friends. Maxwell's delightful description of the steps Mijbil took to wake him up every morning illustrates perfectly the voluntary control Mij exercised on his dental armoury. Waking with a strange, alarm-clock precision at twenty past eight each day, Mij would try the soft approach first, nuzzling Maxwell's face with little squeaks of 'good morning'. If that didn't do the trick, Mij was left with no other choice than to inject a little force into the situation. He could not fathom the strange affliction of humankind to waste good romping time in perpetual slumber. To Mij, it was a travesty of otter law and had to be dealt with by removing all layers of thermal insulation from the sleeping body.

> This he did with the business-like, slightly impatient efficiency of a nurse dealing with a difficult child. He played the game by certain defined and self-imposed rules; he would not, for example, use his teeth even to pinch, and inside these limitations it was hard to imagine how a human brain could, in the same body, have exceeded his ingenuity.

But manage it Mijbil did, by first of all tunnelling under the bedclothes to untuck them from beneath the mattress and then by yanking them off in a series of powerful tugs with his teeth. The pillows were disposed of with as little ceremony. The head and shoulders of the still half-asleep human were tossed into the air and the pillows pulled out in quick succession. 'Left thus comfortless and bereft of both covering and dignity, there was little option but to dress while Mij looked on with an all-that-shouldn't-really-have-been-necessary-you-know sort of expression.'

The amazing thing was that during the entire procedure, Mij did not once resort to nipping, which he undoubtedly knew would have done the job far more quickly. One of Wayre's young otters, Fury, went a stage further. So attached was she to her keeper Barbara that she actually allowed Barbara to take away her food while she was eating, something which rates an entry in *The Guinness Book of Records* as it is a liberty that few carnivores will allow and one that no other captive otter has been known to countenance.

The tidy house-trained habits of otters have already been noted. Captive adults will religiously do their business in one corner of their enclosure instead of leaving deposits in numerous spots as they do in the wild. The absence of regular spraint heaps is probably a result of the limited space of artificial conditions and the fact that there is no need to defend a fenced-in homestead. Whatever the environmental reasons for this modification of wild behaviour, a single loo is certainly convenient for the keeper.

Young otters being raised in the home are just as meticulous about their sprainting habits but Philip Wayre's Kate was an exception. Rather nervous and retiring in nature, Kate went through a tiresome period of ignoring the sand trays with their newspaper surrounds (a containment stratagem for bad aimers) and started to relieve herself in the middle of the living-room sofa or in one of the armchairs. The cause of this lapse in toilet etiquette makes challenging fodder for any Freudian paediatrician but as far as Wayre was concerned it was just plain embarrassing. Guests arriving for dinner would find the Wayres' cushions stripped of their covers and a distinct odour in the air that never quite left the room. Armed with a pile of work one evening, Wayre made himself comfortable on the sofa when he became aware of a cold, sticky wetness permeating the seat of his trousers. Removing both cushion cover and offending trousers, he transferred himself to a nearby chair clad only in underpants, but Kate never did a job without doing it thoroughly and Wayre quickly discovered that chair number two had also been booby-trapped. He ended up doing his work in the one usable chair, naked except for a shirt and socks and looking like some undecided nudist!

The otter's high level of intelligence is revealed in its wide range of activities and retentive memory. It is very innovative in play and generally shows an impressive adaptability of behaviour under captive conditions, working out ways round problems which it would not normally encounter in the wild. In order to make up to Mijbil for the restrictions of his small London flat, Maxwell used to invent games and puzzles that required quite a lot of concentration. Mij took to these entertaining little challenges as readily as he did to his baths with Maxwell. There was one he particularly enjoyed which meant untying a tightly knotted towel to get at his precious terrapin shell, the shell being to Mij what a security blanket is to a child. Mijbil would sit and stare at his human playmate as the cloth coffin was fixed up for the assault. Maxwell would no sooner hand the bundle over than the little statue would come out of his reverie and set upon the knotted lump with Houdini fervour. He would straddle it with his forepaws, sink his teeth into the knots and scuffle all over the room in his efforts to win the contest. Ten or fifteen minutes would see every knot undone and Mij ready for the applause that is the right of all professionals.

Other games which pet otters have been known to play with human companions include 'tiger', 'ambush-the-foot', 'tip-and-run' and 'tug-o-war', but in all these the two-legged team mate has some choice, even if minimal, in opting out. That cannot be said of some of the poor unsuspecting creatures which a mischievous otter might single out for a playmate. Playing ring-the-bell with a bull's tail is a case in point, where the agreement to play is decidedly unilateral. Indeed, the non-cooperation of the bull is essential if the game is to be fully savoured. The bull must be caught napping and the fact that it lashes out with its hooves in an exquisite response of painful surprise adds the required ingredient of danger to the whole event. Like an unsuspecting bull, some of us occasionally have to bear the brunt of an otter's decision to play without our permission and Mijbil's strange predilection for ears easily takes the biscuit. Mij derived a self-contained sort of pleasure out of holing human ear lobes with the precision of a paper puncher. He would give no warning, biting as quickly and neatly as a qualified ear-piercer on the premise that a quick-jab-and-it'll-be-all-over is far more humane than an early warning. The 'game' ended there and Mij would leave the shocked patient and go about his affairs with the air of a contented do-gooder.

When there are no human or animal participants handy, an otter will play by itself, turning the most inanimate of objects into a plaything. Great fun is derived from juggling with pebbles or similar-sized objects and many an adult otter has been induced by this game to forget its ottery responsibilities for a while and don the cloak of clownish infancy. The juggling act is performed with back to the ground and paws frantically bicycling in mid-air. The forepaws do all the work, the hind paws mimicking them with uncontrolled momentum as if connected by a common chassis to the same power source. The clawless otters are particularly adept at this game of legerdemain but this is not to say the European otter is butter-fingered: it can pass two or more marbles from palm to palm for minutes on end without dropping them. And judging by the piles of small shells and rounded pebbles often found in their holts, wild otters seem to indulge just as much as tame ones in juggling games and dribbling sessions. But small objects are not always regarded as toys to throw around and keep in motion. Like Mijbil's terrapin shell, such articles as flowers, fir cones, eggs or dirty bits of rag are often carted around with the reverence of a Moslem handling his prayer beads. The attachment is, however, impermanent, a passing fancy that lasts as long as it takes for boredom to set in—usually just a few hours. The old is then rejected for the new, this being the way an otter ensures a buoyant and healthy interest in the world around him.

Otter intelligence was harnessed in the old days when the animals were trained to hunt for fish in the rivers and seas. The idea originated in south China around AD 600 from where it spread to Malaysia and India and, by the fifteenth century, to Europe. James I was one of the first Englishmen to employ otters as fishing helps in addition to the more traditional cormorants and ospreys. A domesticated otter supported a Swedish family every day with fish, while in Leicester-shire, England, one Nicholas Seagrave reared a female otter which he taught to catch fish and bring them back to him on command. Some stately houses in Sweden are supposed to have kept otters that would catch fish at a signal from the cook.

The practice of using otters in this way is still prevalent in the upper mountainous parts of the Yangtze and its tributaries, in India and in Malaysia where both river and sea fishermen keep packs of up to a dozen trained otters. Many western visitors have seen otters tethered round the waist or neck to bamboo stakes outside their owners' shacks on the beach or leashed to the bows of sampans. The otters are allowed to satisfy their appetites after they have filled the fish baskets but some men still like to keep hold of the leads while the otters do their thing, just in case their thoughts turn to escape. A trained otter is worth as much to a local villager as a trained dolphin is to a marina. Most fishermen get the otters to catch one fish at a time but near Ichang on the upper reaches of the Yangtze they use large dip nets into which a muzzled otter drives all the fish it can. The net is then hoisted up with both fish and otter in it. Sometimes a cord tied tightly round the otter's neck was used instead of a muzzle or leather cups for the canines to prevent the animal from feeding. This method of preserving the fish catch must have been most uncomfortable, if not painful, for the poor otter.

Perhaps more painful for the owners was the process of training their helpers. In 1859, Freeman and Salvin suggested a method which contemporary otter experts have declared they would not like to try themselves. The owner is directed to prevent his otter from eating the fish he has just caught by approaching him quietly and taking hold of his tail in one hand while extricating the fish from his jaws with the other. The intrepid owner is then supposed to reward the apprentice fisherman with small pieces of food, 'after which he will again take to the water in search of more'. No mention is made of the otter doing the rewarding with a quick nip instead of meek aquiescence. E. W. Gudger mentions a few less quixotic schemes in his 1927 article on the use of otters as fishermen in various parts of the world. There was a German in the early 1890s who reckoned that three or four months was the best age for training otters to fish, and that the secret is to start the animal off as a vegetarian, totally excluding raw meat, fish and blood from its diet. Instead, warm milk, cereal, fresh vegetables and fruits should be fed and only in the later stages should the otter have cooked fish. But there is a catch in the finale. The fish, deliberately hot, is offered after a couple of days of imposed fasting and the poor hungry carnivore does the predictable thing and burns his gums. 'If this is repeated a few times, it will forever afterward have a proper awe of biting into scaly creatures.' The next stage of the German's training programme is a lesson in retrieval, first with an imitation leather or oakum fish and eventually with live ones from a pond or stream. The slightest mutilation of the fish and the otter is given the hot-fish treatment or punished with a bucketful of water which the meticulous German feels all otters hate. Before setting off into the country for the first dress rehearsal, we are advised to give our otter a hearty meal in order to reduce the chances of half-nibbled fish.

Another long-winded technique, dating back to 1752, was published by a Johannes Low of Sweden. Again the young otter is forced into vegetarian eating habits. Once accustomed to the new diet, the budding fisherman is also taught to fetch and carry like a dog, but in this case on verbal command. The tools of the trade consist of some form of dummy fish and a potentially pain-inflicting collar attached to a lead. Then comes a repetitive trial-and-error stage in the conditioning drill, in which a pull on the lead and a command of 'Come here' is followed by a 'Lay hold' order, on which the otter must grip the 'fish' in its jaws. Then one calls 'Let go' and twists the spiked collar until the words are obeyed. The 'fish' is then replaced by a real one and finally even the leash and collar can go. The success of the course is guaranteed by incorporating into the last stages a permanent system whereby a qualified candidate is allowed the head of every fish he catches. This is a fail-safe device which panders realistically to the otter's carnivorous appetite.

While life as an indentured fisherman cannot be altogether a bed of roses for an otter, one has to agree with Bishop Heber who wrote in the early 1800s that the simple Hindu shows better taste in taming the otter and training it to fish than 'half the otter-hunting, badger-baiting gentry of England'. And the same disgust must be felt at those lords of the manor in the Middle Ages who used otters as expendable turnspits! Otters have a natural propensity for retrieval and it is this talent which fishermen have channelled and put to productive use. Otters actually enjoy bringing back objects to their masters. It is a game which by its mutual dependence cements the human-otter relationship.

S. J. Hurley put his pet otter's retrieval talent to use during a shoot in the marshes. Any birds that fell in a deep pool or bog hole were sought out by the otter and brought to heel. But Harting took his otter's hunting skills a stage further by teaching him to hunt for his own kind. Sandy, as he was called, was brought up with Harting's pack of otter hounds and would accompany them on every hunt. It was Sandy's job to track his wild relatives and lead the dogs to the holts, a duty he performed with inborn ease because the scent trail was in his own language and not, as it was to the dogs, in a foreign one. Sandy was promoted to leader of the pack after he displayed a streak of initiative one day by voluntarily extending his duties and grabbing the otter quarry by the neck. Armed with all the advantages that 'inside information' bestows on a double agent, Sandy notched up no less than twenty wild otters on his death list. Needless to say, there is something tragic about a non-human animal brainwashed into betraying its own race.

That captive otters have helped men to make a living there is no doubt. There is also no denying that as pets they have given many people infinite pleasure and companionship and at the same time provided some insight into natural otter behaviour. But nothing can better the thrill of seeing one's first wild otter, especially if the sighting is a culmination of long days and nights of patient tracking and waiting in uncomfortable conditions.

8

Looking for the Otter

My first and only sighting of a British otter was back in 1972 when I had decided to earn some money at strawberry-picking during the university summer holidays. As a money-making venture it did not live up to expectations, the ten pence paid out for every 6lb of strawberries picked barely covering food costs and falling short of board expenses. After three days of back-breaking work I decided to call it a day, ate all the strawberries I could pick in the last afternoon and left to explore the broads of Norfolk on foot.

It was very early the next morning that I found myself on the bank of a quiet inlet of the River Yare, sitting on my haunches wondering why I had woken at 2.30am and not been able to get back to sleep again. Whatever the cause—the surfeit of strawberries consumed the day before or the bad dream in which the farmer had buried me alive under a hideous rubble of over-ripe ones—my insomnia had forced me out into the open a good five hours earlier than usual. The pale light of dawn fanned out like a lacewing spreading its wings to dry. It was quiet and windless, the ground was damp and the grass heavy with dew, hence the reason for my sitting Arab-style on the bank. The river flowed black through a misty green expanse of sycamore trees and bramble bushes as I waited for the sun's rays to harden and a plan of attack to resolve itself in my head. A sudden movement in the water about fifty yards downstream caught my peripheral vision. Giving the object the benefit of my full gaze, I saw in the dim light the black muzzle of a real wild otter! It kept disappearing for a few seconds at a time only to resurface as frequently for air, but for all that its movements were smooth and sleek, not jerky like a mink's. I watched in silence as the otter swam diagonally across the width of the river towards the bank opposite me. It was less than thirty yards away and had not yet seen me half-hidden among the bushes. Unfortunately, not being of Arab stock, my knees had begun to feel the strain of nearly fifteen minutes of squatting. I should not have shifted my weight but I had to ease the cramp and although the noise would have been swallowed up in the bustle of the dawn chorus that followed soon after, in the prenatal stillness of early morning it sounded like a firecracker. The otter sank immediately with barely a ripple and failed to reappear during the next hour by which time the day was already too old for any man-fearing otter to be seen abroad.

My delight in seeing a wild European otter is understandable in view of the rarity of such sightings, especially in Norfolk where there are only seventeen otters left compared with what must have been three or four times that number in better times. Even those scientists who have spent many years studying the otter seldom come upon one in the wild. Otter hunters are probably the only people to have made more than just a few sightings but the situation in which they are seen is hardly edifying. Sightings are no problem with the giant otter; this South American species is in fact something of an exhibitionist. Family groups travel around in broad daylight and, if anything, are mildly curious rather than fearful of observers in their territory, periscoping out of the water to get a better look at the 'opposition'. I managed to habituate several family groups to my presence in a canoe in a matter of weeks.

Our native otter is very difficult to glimpse in its natural environment primarily because it is at its liveliest when most god-fearing folk are safe in bed, but seeing one is not impossible. You must be prepared to stay up all night and to remain perfectly quiet and motionless for hours on end. Since otters respond to red light as strongly as they do to ordinary white light, red-filtered torches cannot be used as they are during badger-watching, so you will have to depend on the stars and the moon for illumination. It is best to keep vigil on your own so that you are not tempted to talk. Otters have good ears, and at night there are fewer background noises to muffle whispers. Sleep is the greatest enemy of nocturnal animal watchers so take along a flask of coffee or tea to keep it at bay. Sandwiches are not recommended—it seems virtually impossible to unwrap and eat them without making a noise. Wayre kept a round-the-clock check on the activities of his captive otters and found that peaks occur during the early part of the night and again just before dawn, a pattern which should be borne in mind when planning your night out. Preparation is all-important if success is truly desired. It is important to know the area well and to have done some homework on the local resident otters. As explained a little later, this is done indirectly by studying the animal's tracks, spraints and other signs to find out when they were left (see also Appendix 1). It should then be possible to predict in what part of its territory the resident otter is likely to be at a certain time of the week or month. By choosing a well-concealed vantage point as far as possible downwind of the landing place, spraint heap or holt in use, you will improve the chances of a sighting. Not that success should be expected right away—otter itineraries are notoriously variable—but careful preparation narrows down the possibilities of where to look and keeps unproductive vigils to a minimum.

Should you find a breeding holt in use do not let your curiosity get the better of you but hide a couple of hundred yards away and use binoculars or a telephoto camera lens to magnify the events. Otters are very sensitive to human disturbance and approaching too close or setting up a hide could easily frighten the bitch and cause her to remove her cubs to a safer place. The three virtues to remember are self-restraint, patience and persistence—they eventually pay the highest dividends.

For those of us who find night life a little too strenuous, there is an alternative. On the rocky shores of Scotland's remote west coast, otters can still be seen during the day. Philip Wayre has spent many hours exploring the rugged terrain of north-west Scotland and was rewarded one day with the appearance of an adult bitch bringing a fish to her two cubs who were frolicking with each other on the shore. With the wind in his favour, Wayre managed to get within a few paces of the family group. Kruuk and Hewson have also observed wild otters foraging during daylight hours on the shores of the Ardnish peninsula in Inverness-shire. In these secluded areas which seldom hear the tread of a human foot the otters are bold, but contrary to popular belief some inland populations are equally venturesome. Eighteen years ago Marie Stephens found evidence of otters going about during the day along the River Clettwr in North Wales. She would occasionally

Rare sight of an otter perched on a rock (*centre*), in its natural habitat on the coast of Shetland (*Bobby Tulloch*)

come across very fresh spraint still in its pool of urine which indicated the depositor had been there shortly before her. And, as already mentioned, a farmer in County Westmorland told me that he quite recently came upon an otter in broad daylight swimming near the waterfall at Kirkby Lonsdale; it had apparently surfaced quietly but on seeing the human figure had snorted in apprehension and promptly disappeared again. But, said Frank, there was no doubt it was an otter and what is more, he and his friends have seen other otters during the day along several streams in Lincolnshire.

Exciting as real flesh-and-blood eye contact is, it is by no means essential to see an animal in order to collect data on its movements, behaviour and numbers. A great deal can be gleaned by indirect methods, by looking for and analysing the tracks, signs and droppings

116

of the animal. Scientists like Erlinge, Bannister and Weir, Macdonald and Mason and West, have all unearthed important facts and figures on the otter's distribution, numbers, food habits, daily and seasonal movements and territoriality just by traditional tracking and by collecting spraint at regular intervals, perhaps once every week or fortnight. That said, you still have to know the best areas to look in; it is no use investigating any locality where the water is polluted, the banks cleared of their natural cover and human disturbance extensive. River-bank clearance has a particularly severe effect, because the lack of protective cover is anathema to a mammal as secretive as the European otter. Those areas especially favoured by otters are known as optimal habitats. Sub-optimal habitats are not quite so suitable but still provide adequate cover and food requirements. Optimal inland habitats contain waterways that are eutrophic or high in plant and animal nutrients; sub-optimal habitats contain oligotrophic or low-nutrient waters. Eutrophic areas in England include the Norfolk Broads, the Fenlands, the Hampshire chalk streams, the Sussex rivers and the Somerset levels, though unfortunately most of them have suffered man's interference and are no longer the prime otter counties they once were. In many parts of Britain today the otter has been pushed from optimal habitats to less satisfactory sub-optimal areas.

Whichever river system or piece of shoreline you plump on as a tracking site it is very important to keep disturbance to a minimum. Disturbance is often unintentional but nonetheless if continued over a long period it can result in the otter residents moving out of the area. The Friends of the Earth in their campaign to conserve the otter have compiled an Otter Watcher's Code which, if conscientiously observed, should ensure that the interests of both naturalist and otter remain compatible. I have reproduced, in slightly extended form, FOE's list of do's and don'ts:

1 It is best to go alone and certainly never with more than three people, or there is every chance you will be tempted to talk.
2 Do not trample the undergrowth as the otter relies on this for cover.
3 Do not take a dog with you. It might follow the scent of the resident otter to its daytime hideaway and cause it great stress.
4 Do not annoy any private landowner—ask for permission before walking through private land.

5 Do not remove spraints. You may ruin other people's surveys and upset the otters' olfactory communication system.
6 Do not obliterate otters' footprints as this will make survey work for other people much harder.

Spraints are one of the most distinctive otter features you will come across in the field. When fresh, a single otter spraint appears as one or two loosely constructed black cylinders laid side by side with a total length of ¾-3in (2-8cm) and a diameter of ⅖-⅗in (1-1.5cm). They turn grey with age and Lloyd describes old otter spraint as looking like cigar ash. At this stage they disintegrate easily into heaps of fish scales and vertebrae weathered by the sun and rain. There should be no confusion over what are otter droppings and what aren't. The only other animal that produces anything like them is the feral mink, but mink faeces are thinner, more compact in texture, contain smaller fragments of fish remains, taper more at the ends and have a rather unpleasant smell. With giant otters, smell goes a long way in guiding the observer to the latrines of a family group. Giant otters have large communal spraint heaps on each of their marking sites, and when fresh

Spraint heap consisting of three or four spraints (*Beverley Trowbridge*)

they can be smelt from several hundred yards downwind. Unfortunately for scat-spotters in Europe, the common otter does not spread its faeces in this way, but there *are* certain likely areas to try first which help to narrow the field of search. The first places where fieldworkers like Mason and Weir search for otter spraint are the sandbars and concrete sills beneath bridges. Otters favour these points because they are prominent to transients passing through and are well above the high-water mark. To the surveyor or naturalist, they have the advantage of being easily visible and accessible by car. Once all the bridges have been inspected, the search must continue on foot or by boat. Otters have a strange predeliction for weirs, and a careful search made on both sides where they meet the bank may well reveal a spraint pile or sign heap. Sign heaps are another type of otter 'monument'. They are places where an otter has scraped together little heaps of sand, mud or vegetation and deposited a spraint or drop of scent on top. No one knows if they convey different information from an ordinary spraint, but, whatever their significance, they are very useful indicators of otter presence.

Large boulders and fallen logs in fast-flowing (oligotrophic) rivers may also prove fruitful for spraint, but it is only worth inspecting those that are not likely to be covered by the spring floodwater. There tend to be spraint heaps to one side of most landing places where the otters haul themselves out of the water onto the bank. But undisturbed verges further up the bank should also be searched, especially in winter and early spring when landing-place spraint spots may be flooded out. Surprisingly enough, Wayre encountered otter spraints, as well as their footprints and food remains, in bays of mud made by cattle coming daily to the water's edge to drink. Scats are also regularly deposited in couches or lie-ups hollowed out under the roots of ash and sycamore, outside the entrances of coastal holts and on the triangular tongues of land where two tributaries meet or where a side stream meets the main river. In some areas, during the colder months of the year otter runways can be followed as easily as a rambler's footpath in the country, but in summer the vegetation becomes lush, particularly near the water, making sprainting places more difficult to find. However, scat are actually more noticeable in spring in some parts of an otter's range on account of new green growth sprouting faster from them than from the surrounding ground. Looking for spraint in marshes, both fresh and salt, is hard, foot-slogging work because every drainage canal, ditch and dyke has to be covered if the job is to be done properly.

With the sizeable amount of physical effort involved in scat searching, one is amply justified in asking just how much information scats give us about the otter. Experienced observers can sometimes tell the difference between spraint from one otter and spraint from another and this gives a rough idea of the number of otters in a given area. To differentiate between otter spraints, one must analyse them for parasitic infestations like the tapeworm, or for the remains of a particular meal which are often found in a long series of excrements. Erlinge managed to track individual otters in this way and when combined with observations on the size of otter footprints he got a good estimate of the number of them in the study area. Parasitic infestations sometimes also indicate sub-dominance and certainly one adult male whose scats contained tapeworm remnants was confirmed by Erlinge's direct observations as having a sub-dominant status.

Some hunters profess not only to tell which scat is otter A's and which is otter B's, but also to be able to judge the sex and age of the individual just by looking at the deposit. There are others who claim they can tell in which direction an otter travelled by noting the position of the spraint; if on the downriver side of a boulder or log, the otter has swum past in an upriver direction. One assessment that should not be too difficult for even a novice to make is the degree of freshness of the scat. Black, mucus-covered segments indicate the depositor has passed that way within the last few hours, whereas grey segments or white fragments point to a much earlier deposition, a few days up to several weeks old. By making a regular check of all spraint sites for recent usage, you should be able to construct a rough timetable of otter movements in the study area. As suggested on page 115 this will help you to plan your sessions of direct observation. All scat sites should be recorded as dots or crosses on a large-scale map because the markings will provide some idea of where territorial boundaries are and the size of adjacent territories. Of course this assumes your willingness to patrol several miles of stream and probably several square miles of lake or marsh!

By far the most widespread use of an animal's spraint is to tell us what the animal has eaten. This requires collection of scat samples and their analysis back at base. Scat analysis is best left to the experts because not only does it require an intimate knowledge of all the likely prey species in the area, it also requires the use of a dissection microscope for identification of the more minute bits and pieces. So as FOE advise in their Otter Watcher's code, leave all spraint well alone; there is a great deal of information to be gained by merely noting its freshness and marking its location on a map. However, for those interested in how spraints are treated back in the laboratory, and how the fragments are identified as belonging to this or that animal, a brief rundown is given in Appendix 3.

Tracking otter footprints or seal, as they are sometimes called, gives more immediate information on an individual's movements and, roughly, on otter numbers, than tracking scats which have to be analysed to determine their depositor's identity. In practice, the two methods are used to complement each other. Footprints are also useful for piecing together information on the animal's gait, whether it was walking, running, galloping or sliding at the time. The accuracy of this

Otter footprints on coarse sand (*Beverley Trowbridge*)

method depends on the type of ground underfoot and its consistency. Good substrates for preserving imprints are snow, semi-soft mud and wet sand. On these, otter tracks are well delineated and easy to recognise because the webbing between the toes makes an impression on the ground and gives the print a unique rounded appearance.

Otters have no heel but the round ball under the sole of each foot distinguishes their mark from other mammalian footprints. The claws may or may not show, depending on the consistency of the mud, sand or snow. If the substrate is firm, the claws are seen as tiny 'nipples' attached to the front of the digit indentations. An otter's hindfeet are slightly longer and wider than the forefeet; though the difference is obvious in the prints only if the ground is firm and the impression good. The thumb and big toe do not always make their mark and you end up with four-toed tracks. Mink tracks are rather similar in shape to otter tracks but very much smaller, so really the only other mammal with similar tracks is the coypu, a vegetarian rodent which, like the North American mink, got loose from breeding farms after it was introduced from Argentina in 1930. The most obvious difference is that a coypu's hindfeet are twice the size of its forefeet. (*See* Appendix 1) Should you have real doubts on the owner of some pawprints, reliance will have to be placed on other signs in the vicinity.

In his studies in Sweden, Erlinge would tell the sex and the approximate age of an otter from the tracks. Erlinge would regularly prepare the ground of landing places by smoothing over the mud or sand with water. He assumed that the deepest and largest imprints were made by dog otters. But even given a suitable substratum such as snow, mud or sand (all three of which Erlinge was fortunate enough to have in his study area), this interpretation is not reliable. The depth of any animal's imprint depends very much on the speed at which it is travelling, as this affects the pressure each foot puts on the ground. Moreover, even if a male and female otter move at the same pace on the same substrate the male's tracks are not invariably bigger than the female's.

Philip Wayre took some length and breadth measurements of the forefeet of two captive adult females and one captive adult male on areas of soft mud. One of the females left on average a wider print than the male, who was almost twice her weight! As an additional

Walk
Stride distance: 14 in (36 cm)
Speed: 1–2 mph

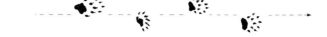

Bound
Stride distance: 31½ in (80 cm)
Speed: 10–15 mph

18 Otter locomotion on land. When walking, there is alternate movement of diagonal fore and hind limbs. When bounding, limbs move in pairs, the hind moving in front of the fore. The corresponding tracks (*after Lawrence and Brown*) are not synchronized

experiment, Wayre extended the experiment to two sixteen-week-old cubs of either sex. Not only did he find the young female prints to be almost 10 per cent longer and wider than those of the male cub, he also noted they were longer and of the same width as the prints of one of the adult bitches already mentioned. So two similar sets of seal seen side by side in the field do not necessarily signify an adult courting pair or even two sub-adult siblings who have recently gained their independence. They could have been made by a bitch and her four-month (plus) cub. On the other hand, three sets of seal are almost certainly the work of a family group. Clearly the moral of the story is to exercise caution in your interpretations of otter footprints. Considering the impressive number of clues they can provide in conjunction with spraint data on otter behaviour, it seems unnecessary to introduce tenuous assumptions.

The pattern in which otter tracks are laid down can tell us something of the individual's gait. There are two aspects to take into account: the striding distance and the position of the hind prints relative to the fore prints. A walking otter has a loping gait, the hind feet being placed behind the tracks of the forefeet. Each stride covers a distance of about 14in (36cm) but this extends to around 20in (50cm) when running or trotting (4-6mph, 6-10kph). Only when bounding or galloping (10-15mph, 16-24kph) do the hind feet fall in front of the forefeet prints, the striding distance increasing to 31in (80cm).

Snow is a very helpful substrate on which to 'read' otter activity. Imprints and slide marks are as clearly revealed on snow as handwriting on a notepad. Typically, there is a shallow scoop between the pad marks of otter seal on soft snow which is caused by the otter's low-slung body. The carriage height of all short-legged creatures is dictated by the length of their legs and for the otter this is less than 6in (15cm). Slides are far more common on snow than on mud and are not confined to the banks, the otters taking advantage of the slightest of inclines to slither along. This indulgence in snow skating is as likely to be a form of play as a means of getting from A to B quickly. Anthony Buxton was certainly convinced that the otter tracks he saw during the severe winter of 1939-40 were the work of an otter 'rollicking home to bed' after a night out on the river. 'Every mound or bank in his path had been climbed for the sake of a toboggan down the other side; into every pool he had dived, and splashed and then rolled in the snow; on every slippery surface he had broken his canter with a series of dashing slides.' Buxton measured the play slides and found they were about 10ft (3m) long and 8in (20cm) or so wide. Each one was smooth and compact throughout, except for the two pad marks of the hind feet where the otter had landed from his mid-air leap to begin the slide and another pair of hindfeet tracks at the end of the slide made as he took off again for the next gallop. Interestingly enough, the slides of this particular otter could have been recognised again because of the way in which the far end of each slide bore a peculiar left-handed curl. In the same way as certain irrelevant movements will characterise the 'style' of a particular tennis player, so the left-handed curl was a trait of Buxton's otter.

Blended together, all these methods of studying the unobtrusive European otter have proved very useful in helping us to discover more about its sociobiology and ecology. And there is still much to be learnt. For example, we do not know the density of fish required to support a resident otter; we know little about what happens to the juveniles after the family group disbands, and even less about the degree of polygamy in male otters and the way in which this is related to the exclusion of fathers in the single-parent families. There is likewise nothing known about the factors operating in habitat selection and how these are influenced by pollution and human disturbance. Studies designed to answer these and other questions are now in hand. The recent nationwide survey has already provided a more precise picture of the population densities and distribution of the otter in Britain: the results were far from heartening.

9

The Hand of Man

The relationship between the otter and man has always been a stormy one, an association steeped in persecution. Most latter-day farmers and freshwater fishermen regarded the otter as a 'subtil' enemy of their interests, a 'destructive desperado', a 'pillager' with 'greedy jaws'. Even the great nineteenth-century painter and ornithologist John James Audubon took on the attitudes of the day: he actually confided in 1826 that his favourite subject for the brush was an otter in a trap. That he preferred to paint an otter confined to a man-made prison and not one swimming free among reeds and boulders is patent testimony to the tradition of bad public relations. It comes as a relief to learn that Audubon changed his attitude toward the otter after keeping two as pets.

Otters were accused of killing salmon, trout and poultry in large numbers, not only to satisfy their own needs but often just for the fun of it. This allegation of mindless carnage was as misplaced as the others. The otter is neither wasteful nor destructive; nearly always it eats all the fish it catches, leaving scarcely a scale for the rats and foxes to scavenge. Indiscriminate killing occurs only under unnatural conditions where there is a glut of prey in a confined space, for example in fish hatcheries or in fish traps set in the river. Until they have learnt to suppress the chase reflex, young otters in captivity do sometimes kill more than they can eat but this is largely because the water is artificially overstocked, and the behaviour is consequently too untypical to warrant criticism. No one can dispute the occasional attack on trout hatcheries by a rogue otter but, as Gavin Maxwell points out, these incidents are as exceptional as attacks on humans by man-eating lions. One such rogue otter had its bent character forced upon it by a trapper. The poor beast had caught one leg in a steel trap and, being unable to swim, was condemned to procure its meals in other ways. If anything, its use of the trout hatchery as a source of food says much for its ability to adjust to new conditions.

The conviction that otters were 'midnight pillagers' that 'swallowed all' is seen in an extract from a letter dated 8 November 1544, from Sir Henry Savile of Tankersley and Thornhill to his cousin of Plumpton.

> The cause of my sending my servant at this time is this. He informs me that in your country there is a man that can kill otters very well; wherefore I send him to get him for a week. I assure you they do me exceeding much harm in divers places, especially at Woodkirk and Thornhill, and lye in small becks. My folk see them daily and I cannot kill them, my hounds be not used to them.

This was by no means the only campaign of its kind. There were many estates that wanted to rid their rivers and 'stew' ponds of the otter pest.

Misdirected the bulk of the accusations may have been, but when people find a scapegoat they attack with a vengeance. Every hand was raised against the otter. Traps, guns, dogs and sticks, or any other implement that came to hand, were used in the war. The law supported extermination of the otter as far back as the sixteenth century. Millais tells us that otters were so abundant in 1557 around the River Yare in Norfolk that a ruling was passed by the Norwich Assembly compelling every fisherman in the area to keep a dog to hunt the otter. The penalty for failing to do so was a fine of 10s, a crippling sum in those days. Some ten years later another Act was approved, this time by the central government, to include all counties: the 'Acte for the preservation of Grayne' empowered parish constables and church-wardens to offer bounties for heads of animals classified as vermin. Innocent creatures like urchants (hedgehogs), weevils (weasels), armyne (stoats), foulmarts (polecats), greys (badgers), foxes, wilde cats and bowsons (otters) were condemned to death under this category. Imagine the otter, a carnivore, classed as a grain eater!

The bounty handed out for each otter's head varied from 6d to 1s depending on the county. The sum was considerably handsomer than that paid out for some of the other 'villains'. From records kept of the number of otter heads collected, C. A. Howes estimated that between thirty-five and forty animals were killed every year in South Yorkshire alone from the inception of the Act in 1566 until well over a century later. Actually, it is likely that many more otters were killed than the bounty records showed because no account was taken of the animals that managed to get away but died later as a result of their wounds. The eradication programme produced the results everyone wanted— the slow-breeding otter was severely affected, its numbers started to decline rapidly and continued to do so under increasing pressures from humans. The 'Grayne Act' was only the beginning.

According to C. A. Howes, the invention around 1610 of the English lock, a safety device on early firearms, did much to harm the otter by encouraging the use of guns for sport. Further improvements produced more sophisticated models and, by the late 1700s, shoots had become extremely popular. The otter was among the many wild animals that provided a challenging target, hunters being motivated by little other than sport or pest extermination. Only infrequently was the European otter sought for its pelt or its meat, though some Roman Catholics in Europe had a habit of eating it during Lent because they reasoned that, as it lived on fish, its flesh was equivalent to fish flesh!

Few accounts were published at the time on the downward trend of the otter in Britain. The earliest comment on its status was made in 1885 by Hutchinson, who stated that the species had become rare in Derbyshire. In 1896, Lydekker added that otters were rare in Leicestershire, Rutland and Hertfordshire but were still abundant in the remote rocky areas of Somerset, Devon and Monmouthshire, and also in the streams and lakes of Westmorland and Cumberland. Around this time they were suffering 'incessant persecution' from pelt trappers in North Scotland where, today, commercial trapping still goes on.

Despite the buffetings of eradicator and pelt hunter, the otter may well have held its ground and maintained its numbers at a lower level but the threats to its survival did not stop there. There was the Industrial Age to contend with. Steam-powered factories produced, for the first time in history, large quantities of harmful waste. Few animals, including man himself, came off unscathed by such pollution, least of all the otter. Whole populations of the species were driven from favoured habitats to sub-optimal locations, not only through water pollution but also through loss of habitat due to the building of factories and homes for the working community. By the early 1900s, the otter was nothing like as common as it used to be, but many people like Millais and Matthews still reckoned it existed in most counties in Britain and even in small numbers on the River Thames. After both World Wars, otter numbers showed a marked decrease, due probably to increased trapping for the pelt trade, but a recovery came a few years later on both occasions.

The first survey to be conducted on the otter in Britain was by Marie Stephens in 1952, her report being published five years later. She was appointed field investigator to a committee set up to look into the status of the otter in England, Scotland and Wales. The project was funded by various natural-history organisations, a gesture which revealed the extent of concern felt by the scientific community for the first time. Stephens began her report by saying that 'Although far more numerous in the British Isles than is generally realised, otters are rather sparsely distributed.' She made use of the various river-board authority boundaries which in some areas, but not all, correspond with county boundaries. The bulk of information came from interviews with local inhabitants and from her own observations of otter spraints and signs. Facts and figures from otter hunters made up the rest. The interview method had some serious drawbacks. For one thing, cooperation was not always forthcoming and in places where it was, the reports were often conflicting. Moreover, in some areas the informants were unaware of otters living under their very noses. In one village where Stephens was told no otters had been seen or heard for over twenty years, she discovered shortly afterwards several fresh spraint directly beneath the village bridge. The inhabitants had been totally oblivious to these signs which indicated that the river running through the village was in fact a well-patrolled otter territory.

Despite the distortions and the subjective nature of much of the data, Stephens managed to build up a picture of the otter's distribution in Britain. What she found was not all that depressing. There were areas of local depletion such as Bristol, Merseyside and the industrial districts of the Midlands, but in most other areas the otter was described as 'common' or 'very numerous'. Scotland was one of the better areas, as it contained the largest reservoir of otters in both coastal and inland habitats.

But in the decade that followed Stephens' 1957 report, threats to the otter escalated. Pollution increased to unprecedented levels with the popular use of fertilisers, weedkillers and pesticides. More and more of the otter's habitats were encroached upon by the spread of towns, factories and roads, by the dredging and canalisation of rivers, by river-authority policy of cleaning riverbanks of trees and shrubs, by fishery managements substituting trout for coarse fish in long stretches of river and stream and by the drainage of marshes. (Alfao had reported in 1898 a gradual emigration of otters from the fens to the broads as the former were being drained for agriculture and development.) People also played more—they could now afford to. One-time minority pursuits like angling, sailing and power boating now came within the scope of almost everyone's purse. Otter hunts also continued to be as popular an institution as ever with the country gentry, though fewer packs of otter hounds were operating in the 1960s than at the beginning of the century (13 and 21, respectively). To what extent any of these factors was affecting the otter's survival was unknown at the time but there were growing fears of a serious decline in most parts of the country and especially in the south since Stephens' investigation. The apprehension was real and could not be ignored.

In 1968, the Fauna Preservation Society and the Council for Nature asked the Mammal Society to survey the current status of the otter in England, Wales and southern Scotland. The findings were published in 1969 and confirmed everyone's worst fears: 'There appears no doubt that over the southern part of Great Britain there has been a very considerable decrease in the otter population (between 1957 and 1967).' The author outlined a number of possible causes: the increase of fishing, riverside recreation and bankside (riparian) clearance. These activities he considered to be the permanent and inevitable consequence of more people having more time and money to use as they wished, but he also pointed out two other factors of a temporary nature which may have had something to do with the otter's decline: the severe winter of 1962–63 was one and the sudden upsurge in the use of seed-dressing insecticides. It was perhaps significant that the areas where otter populations were most affected were corn-growing areas. But until further studies could be made no one could say for certain if just one, a few or all of these factors had caused the decline and it was suggested that meanwhile otter killing should be halted and attempts made to reduce pollution wherever possible. That way, the otter would be given a fighting chance to recover its numbers in some degree and perhaps to adjust its behaviour to the harmful effects of human activities.

Every scientific study has at least one Achilles heel and the Mammal Society's survey was no exception. The survey relied almost exclusively on figures obtained from eleven otter hunts around the country, only a small fraction of the data being derived from direct and indirect observation made by individuals and river authorities. The Master of every otter hunt keeps an annual record of the number of otters found and killed during so many days of hunting. Expressed as the number of otters found or killed per 100 hunting days, some measure is obtained of the trends in otter populations from one year to the next. The method sounds straightforward—a nice, neat way to find out what is happening on the otter front in various localities. But, as Macdonald and Mason point out, 'hunters are unlikely to hunt in areas which they know to be unprofitable, while they are likely to increase the frequency of visits to rivers which they know to contain otters, leading to an inflated estimate of abundance.' They conclude that it is therefore quite possible to record the same annual hunting success on a continuously declining population. O'Connors suggested inspecting the Masters' diaries to see if hunters do in fact avoid low-otter areas in preference for high-density areas but neither he nor anyone else has followed up the suggestion. Chanin and Jefferies list other deficiencies in the hunt-figure method but stress that it has the advantage of being the only one which provides a picture of past otter numbers, that is from the beginning of the century to after the Second World War. Other field methods give a more accurate census of present numbers but have no figures from the past for comparison.

A repeat study was carried out five years after the Mammal Society's 1968 survey. Hunting data was again used in the same way. The coordinator was again Professor H. R. Hewer, who died shortly after the project was completed but not before he had written the first draft of the report. The results, published in 1974, showed that there had been little change in most of the otter populations around the country since the last study and that three areas had actually shown a slight increase—the Border counties, the Pembroke/Carmarthen area and Dartmoor. A decline was evident only in the East Midlands: Buckinghamshire and Lincolnshire. Hewer believed the localised decrease was due in large measure to human disturbance and the excessive river pollution in this part of the country. On the flat land there the river currents are extremely slow, which does nothing to ameliorate a water-pollution problem. All in all, however, the Hewer report was not pessimistic; it claimed the otter had held its own remarkably well in most parts of the country in the five years from 1968 to 1973. But later analyses and surveys did not come up with quite so happy a conclusion.

In 1978, Chanin and Jefferies published some alarming findings of their investigation on how the otter in Britain has fared through the century. Like Hewer and the Mammal Society, they used hunting statistics to compare large-scale population trends in the first half of the century with the otter's status in the late 1970s, but lumped the figures into five-year averages in order to iron out irrelevant year-to-year variations of hunting success. They found that hunting successes in south-west England rose between 1907 and 1956 (perhaps due to reduced persecution during this period) and remained fairly constant over the rest of the country. However, after 1957, the kills dropped sharply in most of England and southern Wales. The decline was also seen in the north of England and Wales and in southern Scotland but to a lesser extent. In effect, Chanin and Jefferies' results agreed essentially with those of Stephens for the period up to 1957 and with those of the Mammal Society for the interval between 1957 and 1968. However, the trend they described for the subsequent decade was quite different from the one Professor Hewer had inferred. Chanin and Jefferies found that the sudden decline which began in the mid-1950s continued into the 60s and late 70s. There was nothing to indicate a stabilisation of otter numbers in the five-year period 1968–73, and certainly there were few signs of the local increases Hewer talked about. The investigators of the 1978 study examined Professor Hewer's original notes in an attempt to understand the discrepancy between the two conclusions. They found a few inconsistencies which, together with their own slightly different treatment of the hunting data, explained the rift in opinion. Scientists well know that the same data can be drawn up and interpreted by two researchers to produce two rather different end-results. This may be construed as a wry comment on scientific methodology, but in something as important as a wildlife survey where the verdict may be used by a government to decide whether or not the animal concerned should be assured legal protection, it is extremely important to find out who is nearer the mark. Not everyone is prepared to err on the side of caution and give the allegedly endangered creature the benefit of the doubt. There are the inevitable economic interests at stake in addition to the conservation issue and the two are seldom easily reconciled.

Chanin and Jefferies were certainly more cautious in dealing with and interpreting the hunting figures, so it is reasonable to place more reliance on their conclusions from the 1968–73 data than on Hewer's. That said, how can we explain the decline in otter numbers since the mid-1950s? There must have been a sudden change of circumstances: was it that man-made pressures had reached a critical threshold or was some unidentified single factor operating? Chanin and Jefferies ruled out the first possibility since it was difficult to imagine combined factors reaching a critical level simultaneously over a wide area. They then looked at each of the problems affecting the otter separately to see if any on its own could have caused the sudden decline. There was certainly no sudden upsurge in the destruction of the otter's habitat in the mid-1950s, nor an increase in hunting, trapping or accidental otter deaths around this time. Disturbance through water-sports activities could not be the answer because in some areas, such as Devon and Cornwall, disturbance was much less than in others like the Norfolk Broads and yet both localities experienced the decrease in otter numbers at the same time. There was likewise no evidence for supposing disease or the severe winter of 1962–63 to be guilty of such widespread killings—prolonged winters are, after all, normal in the European otter's northern range. And, as detailed in the next chapter, work in Britain and Sweden has dispelled the myth that the introduced mink should be condemned for the otter's falling numbers.

Only one factor was left—pollution. There has never been any shortage of this since the start of the Industrial Age and after the Second World War, pesticides and other chemicals gained commercial momentum. But in 1955 a new form of pollution arrived on the British scene. It was a family of organochlorine insecticides—dieldrin, aldrin and heptachlor—which farmers used as cereal-seed dressings and as a sheep-dip to combat skin parasites. Like the older and more familiar organochlorine insecticide, DDT, which was developed during the Second World War and used widely in agriculture soon afterwards, dieldrin was not poisonous only to insects. The sudden population decline of the peregrine falcon prompted Jefferies and Prestt to analyse bodies for traces of dieldrin; the tests revealed lethal levels of it, which signified a rapid accumulation within the birds' bodies. The two investigators attributed this and the consequent deaths to the ingestion of a few highly contaminated prey rather than to the sub-lethal effects wrought by DDT on both birds and mammals. While quick to develop after exposure, sub-lethal effects take much longer to bring about a population decrease. For example, there was a lag of some ten years between the visible sub-lethal symptoms of thin eggshells in the peregrine falcon and the sparrow hawk and the depressant effect on their numbers. With dieldrin, however, death was almost immediate for avian and mammalian carnivores, as a result of concentration of the residues in the food chain. Taylor and Blackmore reported many fox deaths in the East Midlands during the spring of 1960 and it was later demonstrated that they were almost certainly due to organochlorine seed-dressings, particularly dieldrin, to which foxes are extremely sensitive. Badgers also fell like ninepins between 1961 and 1968, suffering immediate deaths caused by lethal doses and also the sub-lethal effects of fewer pregnancies and spontaneous abortions.

Chanin and Jefferies also found the plummeting of otter numbers from 1957 onwards fitted into this pattern of dieldrin usage. Those areas where the otter had all but vanished coincided with the areas of heavy seed-dressing application—the more southern and eastern counties of Britain. The fact that in the north and west of the country dieldrin was mainly used just as a sheep-dip fits in with the observation of fewer otter and other wildlife casualties in the north and border counties. Tests on the carcasses of otters killed by vehicle and fishing-trap accidents showed they were among the sorry circle of wild animals known to be accumulating significant quantities of dieldrin in their tissues. Twenty-five out of thirty-one otters examined between 1963 and 1973 by Jefferies and his colleagues contained measurable quantities and one animal contained a lethal dose (13.95 parts per million wet weight in the liver). And, as in the case of the badger, this finding fits in with Cranbrook's observations of a shortage of otter cubs during the 1960s.

Although dieldrin was also used in Northern Ireland and Eire for agricultural and industrial purposes, there is nothing to indicate a parallel decline in otter numbers around 1956. Evidence against it came from data collected by two Irish zoologists, O'Rourke and Fairley, in addition to the hunting records of the Brideview and Blackwater Otter Hounds and the annual bounty kills organised by the Foyle Fisheries Commission. Residues of the chemical were found in much of Ireland's wildlife but according to Eades not at high enough levels to cause large-scale fatalities. It seems that dieldrin was not used with quite so heavy a hand in Ireland as it was in the south of England.

Concern was voiced in Britain as the toxic side-effects of the organochlorine insecticides became apparent and there were calls from conservationists and the medical profession to ban or at least impose restrictions on dieldrin and aldrin. The government responded in 1962 by banning the use of dieldrin as a seed-dressing for spring cereals. In 1966, its use as a sheep-dip was also stopped and much later, in 1975, it was banned as an autumn/winter seed-dressing. Dieldrin has few agricultural uses now, though the woollen industry still uses it for moth-proofing carpets and blankets.

Why, however, if the dieldrin-based insecticides were responsible for the otter's decline, has the species failed to recover in the affected areas since the major restrictions in 1962 and 1975? According to Brown, peregrine-falcon populations did start to recover in the years that followed the bans. Chanin and Jefferies suggest a number of possibilities and are currently investigating them. First of all, dieldrin's use in industry (and the consequent contamination of waterways far from the source of release) was not reduced at the same time as its use in agriculture; secondly, the industrially and agriculturally used polychlorinated biphenyls (PCBs) continue to be used in large quantities since their first application in 1930—several hundred tons a year during the last decade for pesticide spraying alone. PCBs have been shown to accumulate in freshwater fish and, not surprisingly, are found in particularly high concentrations in fish-feeding birds such as the British heron *Ardea cinerea*. Because otters, too, eat mainly fish their tissues may well contain high levels of these chemicals. PCBs may not have triggered the 1957–58 otter decline but they may be keeping the numbers low.

Thirdly, in the twenty years or so since the start of the decline, there has been immense habitat destruction and disturbance of banks and waterways, and the otter may be finding reoccupation extremely difficult if not impossible, especially in those areas where the landscape has become split up through the spread of urbanisation. Fourthly, dieldrin may have been to the otter what the white man is to the South American Indian—the cause of population fragmentation leading to inviability. Otter numbers may have dropped so low that populations have become dissociated into small islands, unable to communicate or interbreed with one another. Under such circumstances, recovery would be a slow, difficult process and any mortality factor such as hunting or road accidents which used to be insignificant would now be enough to keep the population down. Last of all, there is the mink to consider. Although scientists now feel it did not actually *cause* the otter slump (see Chapter 10), perhaps its spread, like that of humans, is deterring the otter from recolonising old habitats.

Since Chanin and Jefferies' assessment of the otter's status in Britain, two major surveys have been conducted. Neither of them depended on hunting data, reliance being placed instead on fieldwork in which otter spraint and other signs were looked for. The Mammal Society Survey, co-ordinated by Dr Paul Chanin of Exeter University, was carried out in England between 1973 and 1979. The National Survey Programme (NSP), which included Wales and Scotland in addition to England, was much shorter, lasting from 1977 to 1979 and was co-ordinated by Dr Don Jefferies of the Nature Conservancy Council. A speedy survey was important with an endangered animal like the otter whose overall status appeared to deteriorate from year to year. Both surveys used a similar method (*see* figure 20) but the

136

Mammal Society Survey relied on 40-50 lay volunteers whereas the National Survey Programme employed a few experienced fieldworkers (one for England, two for Scotland and three for Wales). The decision to use a few experts was made after Dr Chanin realised that the volunteer method was proving unreliable. In the first place, it was difficult to get enough workers and many of those that stayed the course succumbed to the temptation of ignoring 'negative' areas where otters were generally thought to be absent.

Briefly, the method used was to divide up each country into 10km (6.2 miles) squares using the national grid: in each square about 6 survey sites were selected. The likeliest otter areas were chosen, the only stipulation being that the sites had to be at least 5-8km (3-5 miles) apart. At each of the six sites, the surveyor searched the river banks for signs of otters. The maximum length of riverbank, lake shore or coastline searched was 600 metres (656yd). If no otter spraint or tracks etc were found, the site was marked as 'negative', but as soon as a sign was found it was marked as 'positive' and the search in that site was terminated even before the 600m had been covered.

By mapping each 10km square as 'negative' (ie, all six sites bare of signs) or 'positive' (ie, at least one site with a sign), it was possible to get a good idea of otter *distribution*—or presence/absence—in each country. In addition, the *relative densities* in various areas could be compared using the percentage of positive sites in 50km (31 mile) square areas. This measure will reveal any national and regional trends in otter populations when the surveys are repeated in three to five years' time.

England's much greater size meant that the NSP's survey had to be conducted half as intensively as in Wales and Scotland if it was to be completed in time. The surveyor covered 10km square areas and investigated approximately six sites in each, as described above, but only 50 per cent of all the squares comprising England's land surface were looked at. Representational results were ensured by systematic selection.

The outcome of the National Survey Programme justified long-expressed anxieties over the otter's plight in England and Wales. Of the 1,030 sites surveyed in Wales, only 20 per cent showed any signs of otters; while the figure for England was even more alarming—a mere

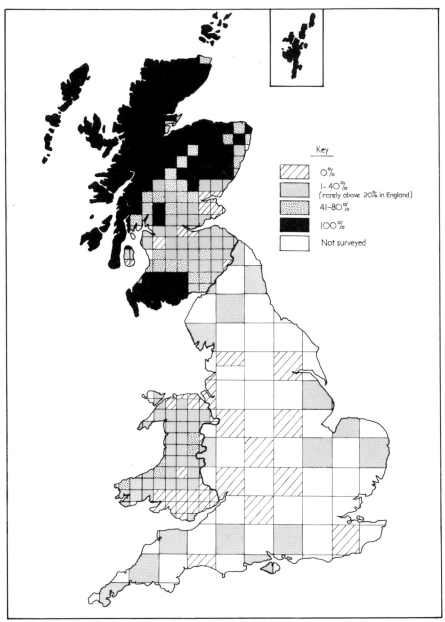

19 Otter densities in Britain 1980—shown as a percentage of positive sites in 20km square tetrads (Wales and Scotland) and 50km square tetrads (England)

6 per cent of the 2,940 sites visited were positive. The hardest hit areas, where otters were absent or sparse, were north and south-east Wales and the central part of England. Otter densities were highest in mid- and south-west Wales, the Welsh/English border, Devon, Cornwall and Northumberland. Although East Anglia and several other counties contained otters, the densities were generally so low that the viability of the populations was seriously in doubt. The Scottish results were much better, as expected. A total of 4,636 sites were searched and 73 per cent proved positive. The lowest densities coincided with areas of high population—the eastern and central lowlands and the southern uplands. In these parts, otter populations showed signs of fragmentation or isolation, the first symptoms of ex- tinction. Predictably, otters were most abundant along the northern and north-western coasts of the mainland and among the off-shore islands. Many of the 10km squares in this important otter habitat con- tained all-positive sites, indicating a well dispersed, healthy population.

On the face of it, the Mammal Society Survey produced a more optimistic picture of the otter's status in England. Records were received from 596 ten-kilometre squares, though these were not as evenly spaced as the 600 that were surveyed for the National Survey Programme. Of the 2,057 sites investigated, 30 per cent were positive, considerably more than the 6 per cent figure derived by the NSP for England. This discrepancy between the two surveys can be explained by certain differences in the methods used. The Mammal Society Survey probably overestimated positive otter signs because the volunteer surveyors tended to concentrate on areas where the animal was known to be present, often neglecting 'uninteresting' watercourses that were devoid of otters. The NSP, on the other hand, tended to underestimate the level of otter activity for two reasons. First, sites were selected along *all* river systems and not simply those that were likely to support otters. Secondly, the vast majority of sites were visited on one occasion only (in contrast to repeated three-monthly visits by the Mammal Society Survey) which meant that spraints which may have been washed away by floods or heavy rain would have gone unnoticed. Moreover, the 600m observation lengths at each site provided a good index of otter activity only in areas

A | 1 Site No: 50 | 2 Site Name: Rhosman (Dulais/Tywi) | 3 Grid Reference SN 647242

B | 1 Recorder: | 2 County: Carms Dyfed | 3 Altitude: 30m | 4 Date of Visit: 5.7.77

C HABITAT TYPE	Sea Coast	Sea Loch	Estuary	Lowland Lake / Broad	Upland Loch/ Tarn	Reservoir	Running Water ✓	Bog/ Marsh	Canal

D SHORE TYPE	Boulders	Stones	Gravel ✓	Sand	Silt	Earth ✓	Rock Cliffs	Earth Cliffs

E CURRENT	Rapid	Fast	Slow ✓	Sluggish	Static

F WIDTH	<1m	1 – 2m	2 – 5m ✓	5 – 10m	10 – 20m	20 – 40m	>40m

G MEAN DEPTH	<0.5m	0.5 – 1m ✓	1 – 2m	2 – 3m	3 – 5m	>5m

H VEGETATION	Bankside Vegetation D	Emergent	Floating Attached	Free Floating	Submerged

J LAND USE BORDERING	Bankside Trees S	Upland Grass- land	Permanent/ Temp Grass- land ✓	Mixed/Broad- leaf wood- land	Conifer Woodland	Acid Peat Bog	Arable	Salt Marsh	Heath	Urban/ Industrial	Garden	Fen

K BANK TREATMENT	Canalised	Maintained ✓	Wild	None

L WEED CONTROL	Mechanical	Chemical

M WATER USE	Water Abstraction	Boating/ Powered	Boat/ Sail	Boat/ Manpower	Bank/ Angling ✓	Bankside/ Shooting	Keepered	No use	Reserve

N POLLUTION	UNPOLLUTED	DOMESTIC		AGRICULTURE			INDUSTRIAL			
		organic ✓	others ✓	organic	pesticide	fertiliser	organ -ic	toxin	solid	temper- ature

P MINK SIGNS	Present ✓ Tracks Absent	
Q OTTER HUNTING	Yes No	

R FISH (Species present) G – salmon, sea trout, brown trout

C – eels, gudgeon

S APPARENT DISTURBANCE FACTOR 3 cattle

private fishing

walking

Description or sketch of Site R. Dulais just before confluence with
Tywi. Gravel bed; shallow except for occasional pool.
Gravel fronts much of earthy bank (in parts maintained by
sandbags). Thistles, nettles and grasses densely cover bank,
(though trampled, in parts, by cattle) with some alder and
hawthorn.
So, ample cover; a few exposed tree-roots.
One new road bridge; one small railway bridge. Also the
river confluence

Distance surveyed 1000 m

Description or sketch of sprant sites	Otter signs seen (and number)
Top of large boulder, rectangular in shape (approx. 75 cm × 60 cm, standing 25 cm high) below single-track railway bridge. Boulder probably left from bridge building i.e. not natural. One of a dozen or so boulders left standing on the bank, clear of the water (at present) beneath the bridge. This area very trampled by cattle.	Three sprants on one boulder
	Salmonid ova in sprant

20 a & b National Survey Programme specimen record sheet

where the animals were fairly numerous. In low density waterways otter signs may have been missed by the NSP surveyor and this would have led to an underestimate of actual activity—in the case of the Mammal Society Survey, the repeated visits made by the volunteers would have helped to remove this bias.

When searching for otter signs, notes were made on several environmental features within each site—the level of pollution, disturbance, dredging activity etc and the presence or absence of mink. The data will be analysed by computer and it is hoped that the results will help otter conservation by highlighting its habitat requirements and by identifying the factors that are presently limiting its numbers.

Plans are well in-hand to supplement the findings of the National Survey Programme with more intensive surveys at a local level. For example, the Society for the Promotion of Nature Conservation is presently co-ordinating a survey in England to fill in those 50km square 'gaps' that the NSP scientists were compelled to leave. Local conservation trusts and other naturalist organisations are also formulating plans for intensive surveys along river systems in their districts.

Some independent surveys were carried out several years ago and their findings will provide important baselines for repeat surveys. In Norfolk and Suffolk, the actual number of otters was estimated by a detailed count of their spraints along all banksides and the figure was compared with potential number of otters that the habitat could sustain. Ecologists call this potential the 'carrying capacity' of a particular habitat. For the otter in Norfolk and Suffolk, it was calculated by taking an approximate yardstick of 'healthy' otter density as one pair per 10km (6.2 miles) of stream. The difference between the actual number of otters and the carrying capacity gave an indication of how badly under par was the actual otter population. On such a scale of wellbeing, East Anglia's otters rated poorly.

R. B. West estimated that in Suffolk between 1967 and 1972 there were roughly 36 otters. The county fell into three categories according to the degree of habitat deterioration; some areas still held viable populations, others appeared to be just about in balance and a few sectors were completely devoid of otters. In Norfolk, Sheila Macdonald and Chris Mason estimated 34 otters in 1974–5, far below

142

the carrying capacity of the area, which they calculated to be between 104 and 105. Otters were resident in only about five rivers and there was evidence that the population had become split into a few isolated pockets, the separate groups standing little chance of coming into contact with one another to reproduce. Even more telling was the now total lack of otters on the River Waveney, the boundary river between Norfolk and Suffolk. West had found evidence of otters there three years previously; their rapid disappearance proved beyond doubt that the otter was on a dangerous course in these parts.

Macdonald, Mason and Coghill carried out a similar survey in 1977 along the River Teme and its tributaries in western England and eastern Wales. They found signs of a mere 10 or 12 otters along 213 miles (343km) of stream and river, a population which barely represents a sixth of the area's carrying capacity. Pollution could not be blamed in any of the three localities, because the waterways are all fairly clean by today's standards, especially the Teme river system. The factors responsible here are the rise in popularity over the last two decades of angling, boating and rambling, and the practice of bank clearance by river authorities. With bank clearance, weeds are cut and trees felled in order to improve water flow and reduce flooding, but in so doing, otter holts and hideouts are destroyed. This can mean that a whole stretch of river, rich in fish, is no longer available to the resident otter because of the lack of protection for eating, grooming, resting and concealment. The destruction of oak, ash and sycamore trees was particularly significant: Macdonald and Co found that their loose, extensive root systems were especially favoured by otters for holt construction. On the other hand alder and willow were rarely used.

Independent otter surveys of the Somerset levels and the Exmoor National Park came up with findings that fit in with those of the NSP. The same applies to the only other regional survey. Between 1972 and 1975, the Universities' Federation for Animal Welfare asked Marie Stephens (now Mrs Kind) to supervise surveys in two areas in Wales. In one, a 3km (1.8 mile) stretch of the River Clettwr, otters were still being hunted at the time of the survey. In the other area, the middle section of the River Usk in Breconshire, otter hunting had been banned since 1969. A high level of otter activity was recorded along the River Usk, but on the Clettwr in 1973 Mrs Kind found only a

Pair of otters pictured among the rocks of Shetland (*Bobby Tulloch*)

twentieth of the spraint she had encountered on the same river in 1953. Pollution was not to blame—the water quality was tested and found to be satisfactory. It seems more likely that the sharp fall-off in otter activity was at least partly due to disturbance by the Hawkestone Otter Hunt in the surrounding tributaries of the River Teifi.

As it stands, the otter's strongholds in Britain are the Scottish off-shore islands, northern and north-western coasts; central and south-western Wales; the Welsh/English border; and the extreme south-west and north-east of England. How long these places remain havens for the otter will depend on our attitude to wildlife in general and the priority given to its conservation. Even an island as remote as Shetland is not safe from wildlife disasters—in December 1978 there was a massive oil spill from the tanker Esso Bernica at the Sullom Voe storage terminal. Because of the inadequacy of containment precautions, at least 14 coastal-dwelling otters in Shetland were killed and 18 others were seen oiled but still alive, though not expected to survive. Oil probably destroys the insulating properties of otter fur and may also cause poisoning, through grooming and the ingestion of

144

oiled sea birds. As long as the terminal continues its operations, there exists the possibility of another similar accident in the future.

Elsewhere in Europe the otter is in equally bad straits, for more or less the same reasons. Persecution through the centuries has given way to the modern ills of pollution, habitat encroachment, river management and recreational disturbance. And, incredibly, some anglers and water bailiffs retain the legacy of bygone days and continue to shoot otters in the belief that they are protecting their sport from marauders. A census in West Germany carried out in 1965 reported a total of barely 200 otters left, while in East Germany a 1977 survey estimated a population of 400-800 animals. In the same year, an assessment undertaken in Norway came up with a figure of 550 otters, but even worse was the plight of the species in Switzerland and Italy, in each of which less than 100 individuals remain. Like the British, the Swiss used to have the otter on their list of verminous animals on account of its supposed detrimental effect on sport fish numbers. But they learnt from Poland's mistake of trying to eliminate the otter and finding that the coveted fish species actually declined instead of proliferated. The otter is now protected in Poland and in Switzerland; the last bounties were paid out for five specimens in 1946, with protection finally arriving in 1952. It was a step in the right direction but the measure was aimed at stopping otter shoots rather than at containing habitat destruction and pollution. Not surprisingly, the Swiss otter showed no sign of recovery; of the 40 to 60 animals still around at the beginning of the 1950s not one survived to see through the following decade. A combination of illegal persecution, pollution and burgeoning development put paid to the small advantage gained. Even the exhibits in Zurich Zoo were hounded. During the zoo's first twenty-five years, visitors killed three adult otters, one of them being disposed of by a small boy throwing stones!

The otter has suffered as ignominious a fate elsewhere in Europe, though in at least one country the prospects are brighter. Otter numbers in the Netherlands reached an all-time low of 30 to 50 animals in 1942 but thanks to protective measures taken shortly after, the situation improved encouragingly and in 1970 the count had risen tenfold. In France, however, signs of the otter are few. One of the reasons put forward for its disappearance in at least certain parts of this country is the spread of the catfish, *Ameiurus nebulosus*. When the biologist J. Estanove examined a number of dead otters he found some with their stomachs and intestines perforated, and others had been suffocated by the spines of the fish lodged in the palate and lower jaw. However, Richard Fitter disputed the claim: France's otters, he said, were in danger of extinction because of water pollution, as in Italy where Cagnolaro and his colleagues reported a sharp decrease in fish abundance due to water impurity. This seriously compounded the otter's problems in an Italy that had drained its marshlands on a massive scale in the twenties and thirties. Jan Veen in 1975 deduced that the Waterland province of North Holland had only 30-60 otters which he attributed to the lack of sufficient cover. Sam Erlinge found the same factor operating in Finland and Switzerland but reckoned that in Sweden more important influences were water pollution, shooting and, in some rivers of the Scania province, drowning in fishermen's bow nets. The pollution was exceptionally acute in stretches of river below paper mills which discharged large quantities of mercury as a routine part of the manufacturing process. High levels of mercury were discovered in the livers of both otters and mink. This form of direct poisoning together with the de-oxygenation and fish-killing effect of heavy metal pollution, was an effective otter-killer. With the protection of the species in 1968 (apart from around fish-rearing ponds, where shooting is still permitted), the situation could improve, but probably will not as long as pollution is unchecked.

No one can deny that the otter in Europe is now in a bad way, whatever the causes. It is a mammal particularly vulnerable to negative influences of any kind because of its slow rate of reproduction, its late maturity, its dependence on clean water and its need for privacy. Nevertheless, when shooting and trapping were the only ways we harmed otters they were able to survive; now that we have added disturbance, pollution and habitat-destruction they can no longer do so.

It is still widely believed that the spread of the feral mink in Britain and Europe has been the prime destroyer of the otter. This fast-breeding mustelid from North America which escaped by accident into the English countryside some fifty years ago was thought to have put some sort of a stranglehold on the otter, causing it to disappear from many of its old haunts. We now try to separate fact from fiction.

10

The Immigrant Competitor

The fickle world of fashion has been instrumental in the massacre of many animal species throughout the world. There is big business in parting skins from their rightful owners and placing them on the shoulders of preening men and women as a status badge. Tigers, leopards, ocelots, seals and otters are among those mammals whose fur has been, and still is, coveted for coats, stoles, rugs, slippers or for hanging on the wall. On the other hand, fashion has also brought an increase in the population of certain mammalian species through intensive breeding in captivity. The mink was 'lucky' enough to fall into this category. Its accidental escape and subsequent spread throughout Britain and Europe coincided roughly with the otter's decline and led many people to believe it was the major cause of the otter problem. But until recently, no one bothered to investigate these claims. Looking at the newest evidence at hand, what effect has this naturalised denizen of our countryside had and what might it have on the future of the otter?

The mink's native land is North America with a range extending over most of Canada and the USA, almost identical with that of the native species of river otter, *L. canadensis*. Mink actually have more in common with otters physically, behaviourally and ecologically than with some of their genetically closer relatives such as the stoat and the weasel. Like otters, they are largely nocturnal, shy, and for the most part silent. They lead a solitary existence except in the mating season which is in spring, and do not hibernate. But one of the reasons the mink has spread so quickly in foreign lands is because its litters are large—an average of five or six cubs and as many as seventeen on exceptional occasions—and because it grows quickly and reaches sexual maturity quite early in life, being ready to breed around its first birthday. The otter is less precocious, as we have seen, not coming into breeding condition much before the third year of life. Female mink raise their young in holts similar to those a bitch otter would choose: hollow tree trunks, drainage culverts and holes and crevices among rocks. More terrestrial than otters, mink are adept at climbing (they have been seen over 50ft (15m) up in trees) and at hunting small mammals and birds, but they can also swim well with the help of their semi-webbed feet. They have catholic tastes and eat not only land animals such as field voles, wood mice and poultry but also semi-aquatic mammals, fish, shellfish and waterbirds.

Their territorial system is much like the otter's in that members of the same sex are more antagonistic towards one another than towards members of the opposite sex. Territories are defended by regular marking at traditional sites with spraint, urine and a characteristically pungent scent. Dr Rune Gerell at the University of Lund, Sweden, radio-tagged six wild-caught mink, five males and one female, and tracked their movements continuously for two weeks by which time the transmitter batteries had expired. From this and later fortnightly tracking operations, Gerell found that the males were mainly nocturnal at all seasons and that their level of activity was directly related to increasing length of night and decreasing temperature. The female's activity pattern was much more influenced by pregnancy than by seasonal changes. She was least active during pregnancy and most active during the suckling stage when she became largely diurnal. Gerell also found the mink travelled variable distances every night, from 1km to 11km, the upper limit comparing well with the nightly distances otters travel. Unlike otters, mink are preyed on by foxes, buzzards and other predatory birds, though no one knows what impact, if any, they have on the regulation of mink populations.

A mink is no bigger than a domestic cat, about a third the size of a European otter. Adult males weigh around 4lb (1.8kg) and measure just over 1ft (0.3m) from the nose to the tip of a bushy tail, females being half as heavy though not a great deal shorter. In the wild state, the fine, closely packed fur is dark chocolate-brown in colour offset by a white chin-patch. So aesthetically pleasing is the mink's pelt that fur ranches have been set up all over the world with the express purpose of breeding the creature for the clothing market. Thompson estimated

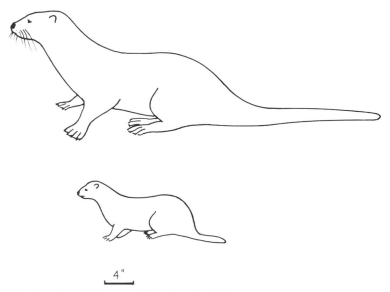

21   Relative sizes of the otter (above) and mink

that in 1959 the world population of captive mink had soared to an amazing 11 million animals. By controlling which individual mates with which, mink have been bred in a variety of colours: palomino, pastel, pearl, topaz, shades of white, and a spectrum of browns, greys and patterned black and whites. Many of the two dozen or so mutants are smaller than normal in size, of reduced fertility and more susceptible to disease, but the fur fashion protects them from the guillotine of natural selection and ensures their continued survival. It is as sophisticated a business of eugenics as breeding dogs or creating new roses, with every now and then a new colour breakthrough being made. Feral offspring of multi-coloured escapees normally revert to the natural dark-brown colour though slight variations are not uncommon.

The facility with which mink escape from their captors must be the envy of every inmate of Wormwood Scrubs. Escapes have been recorded in just about as many countries as introductions were made: Ireland, Scotland, Wales, England, Iceland, Norway, Sweden, Finland and Denmark. They would probably have escaped in Russia too had not their freedom been engineered beforehand: about 16,000 mink were released into the Russian countryside between 1933 and 1970, most of them east of the Urals. On the face of it, it seems a mad scheme and irresponsible to loose an alien species among native fauna without knowing what effect it may have, but the USSR government does benefit by the sale of hunting rights and the taxation of skins.

Britain first introduced mink in 1929 for breeding on fur farms. The predictable escapes occurred and by the mid-1950s mink had become a well-established feature of the English countryside. It was in 1956 on the upper reaches of the River Teign in Devon that breeding in the wild was first noted. Reproductive turnover was as swiftly progressive as oil spreading over water because 1961 saw feral mink alive and well in four counties in England, two in Scotland and one in Wales, a modest area compared with today's distribution of the length and breadth of Britain. The irony is that it was widely believed that escaped mink would not survive for long in the wild. Time proved the pundits wrong and there is now virtually no habitable waterway which has been spared the mink invasion. Ireland has them too, but they have not spread quite so extensively there perhaps because there are fewer farms—none were established before 1950—and fewer escapes. The fact that mink 'moved in' at a time when otters were declining led to the conclusion that the immigrants were driving the otter from its riverside haunts, just as the grey squirrel was blamed for the native red squirrel's chronic decrease: indirect competition was thought to be the problem. There could have been no question of mink actually killing off otters, because the otter is easily four times as heavy and capable of fierce aggression. Indeed, Novikov stretches this point with the rather surprising news that in Russia 'the otter vigorously hunts mink'. The 'anti-minks' reasoned that as mink and otters have a very similar diet of fish and a similar choice in holts, cover, etc, the mink were clearly robbing our native mustelid of a significant portion of its sustenance and prime habitats. It became important, if for no other reason than that the otter's future was at stake, to cease speculation and find out the true relationship between the cousins.

In 1969, the Mammal Society Report of the Otter Committee looked for but found no evidence of feral mink having any untoward effect on otter populations. And as part of his 1973 survey on the otter's status in Britain, Professor Hewer asked each otter hunt a few questions about the mink-otter relationship. The response was skimpy and wholly subjective. Two hunts thought that where mink had become numerous otters had become scarce, and two other hunts supposed that mink might directly kill otter cubs or disturb their breeding holts in some way. Not much in the way of hard evidence, but Hewer did point out the potential value of otter hunts in collecting data on mink numbers. Hunts killed mink as well as otters on their excursions into the country, but they kept no records of the number of kills or finds; if they would do so, said Hewer, the figures could be used to indicate trends in mink numbers in the same way as they were used to assess otter trends. The interaction between the two species could then be analysed. However, this method of collecting information on otter and mink together is now impossible since otter hunting has been banned in England and Wales. Mink hunting goes on, and figures could still be collected on the numbers killed and found, but comparable data for the otter would be lacking.

Recent studies on the effect of the mink on otter populations include Sam Erlinge's in Sweden, Cuthbert's in Scotland and Pavlov's in Russia. Erlinge was the first to tackle the problem and his findings do much to clarify the befogged issue. As in Britain, mink were introduced into Sweden in the late 1920s, and through escapes a thriving feral community was soon established. Swedish otters decreased at around the same time, to much the same pattern as their British counterparts; such similar scenarios in two totally separate countries gave anti-mink arguments added impetus. Leaving aside premature conclusions, however, Erlinge looked at the areas of contact between the two species. The food choices of mink and otter were assessed and the degree of overlap calculated, for summer and winter. Because of its greater dependence on fish throughout the year, it was at once evident that the otter was more adapted to life in water than the mink. The behavioural separation was more apparent in summer, when Erlinge found the otter ate mainly cyprinid fish such as gudgeon and roach, whereas mink preyed largely on nocturnal rodents and crayfish. The otter also took crayfish but to a lesser extent, while both took small amounts of waterfowl. The degree of food sharing worked out at around 30 to 40 per cent of intake in the Swedish river-lake habitat which meant that the competition for food was not nearly as intense as the anti-minks would have us believe.

In winter, when the Swedish lakes freeze, both otter and mink seek open water where fish are more available and easier to catch. The otter again has the aquatic upper hand and makes for the most favourable areas even if this means trespassing on mink-inhabited lakes. The mink are then left to exploit the more difficult ice-prone watercourses. When this situation arises, the mink actually take the initiative to avoid contact with their cousins and depart from the area without fuss, preferring to comply rather than confront. Any feeding ground in winter, whether good or bad, is nowhere near as profitable as in the summer. Prey items are scarce and this is the time that Erlinge found considerable competition develop between the two species, the overlap increasing from the summer 30 to 40 per cent to between 60 and 80 per cent, depending on the area under study. In England, however, there is probably far less competition in winter between the two carnivores because our milder climate does not encourage the formation of ice on streams and lakes. At a time when small mammals are difficult to come by, the mink relies more on fish, and both mustelids tend to eat many more insects and frogs. There are far fewer crayfish around and consequently they hardly featured in either animal's winter diet, especially the otter's. Both species took those fish types that were most abundant and available: pike in one lakeland area, cyprinids in another. On the whole, otter and mink shared many of the food resources but Erlinge noted some minor differences which may or may not have arisen through competition. The otter plumped for the larger specimens of fish (as it did in the summer) and for most of the frogs, whereas the small quantities of birds and mammals taken almost all fell to the mink.

To find out if the arrival of mink had in some way influenced the otter's food habits, Erlinge compared the otter's diet in 1960 with that of the year before, when mink had not yet entered the area. He found the food types and the proportion in which they were eaten were virtually the same in both years so the mink obviously had not forced the otter to modify its menu. And another plank was knocked from under the feet of mink antagonists when the Swedish scientist noticed something else which meant that mink and otter were hardly in the throes of do-or-die competition: there was a distinct spatial separation of the two predators. Otters populated the central eutrophic lakes with wide in- and out-flows whereas mink tended to congregate around the peripheral oligotrophic lakes characterised by stony shores and sparse vegetation, and only sporadically visited high-density otter precincts. There was actually an inverse population relationship: the greater the density of the otter population the sparser were mink numbers and *vice versa*. Only where otter numbers were not over-bearing did mink dare to co-exist and intermingle with them. Erlinge concluded that the otters retained ownership of the habitats they preferred and that as a result, the immigrant minks got what they wanted only some of the time. The otter had first choice and exercised it, whereas the mink had little to choose from and even less to say in the matter. This was the first indication that otters dominate mink rather than the other way round: not all that surprising when you consider the considerably greater size and strength of otters. There is even some evidence of otters taking intimidation a step further: Egorov to a certain extent confirmed Novikov's claim that 'the otter vigorously hunts mink' in the USSR when he found remnants of mink in 7 out of 735 otter scats.

In its native home of North America, the mink coexists quite happily with the local species of otter, *Lutra canadensis*, which is a close relative of our European otter, *Lutra lutra*. The geographical distributions of indigenous mink and otter are virtually identical, extending over most of the continent, and though the interrelationship between the two mustelids there has not been studied in any detail, neither seems to be endangered. Co-existing in a neighbourly sort of way, they do not appear to compete or interfere with each other. This, of course, does not prove that mink are no nuisance whatever to otters in Europe; niche occupation may be similar on the two continents but it is not identical and this could create a mutually adverse interaction wherever the mink lives as an immigrant. But the harmony with which the two live together in North America, in the same habitat, does suggest that mink and otter are not congenitally out-and-out rivals.

Bearing the facts on mink ecology and behaviour in mind, we can now no longer condemn this alien for causing the otter's decline in

Britain and Europe. And this stance is supported by information on the timing of the mink's rise and the otter's fall. A scrutiny of hunting statistics in Sweden and Britain showed that otter numbers began to fall before the big mink explosion. Otter hunts first encountered mink around 1962, several years after the otter decline had begun. Furthermore, Hewer's data on otter observations showed that in two places in Britain where otters had disappeared (Buckinghamshire and the eastern counties) mink were absent, while in other areas where the otter was doing relatively well (for example, Dartmoor and Pembroke and Camarthen) mink were present in fairly large numbers. The otter's annihilation was evidently caused by some other agent or agents (see previous chapter), although it is probable that the contraction of the otter's range made it much easier for the mink to move in, since mink colonisation was generally slowest in those areas well populated with otters. What the mink did was to colonise the optimal habitats which the otter used to inhabit before it was ousted by manmade factors. Being more ecologically versatile than the otter and more tolerant of disturbance, mink can quite happily live away from water if food is abundant and can occupy a wide range of inferior habitats by making do with whatever is available at the time. The big question is, if otter numbers improve and the species tries to recolonise its old haunts will it be able to do so easily or will the presence of mink hem it in and limit recovery? The well-established mink might act as a deterrent and prevent the otter from penetrating their ranks. We must leave it to scientists like Chanin and Jefferies to try to predict the outcome before events reach that stage.

There was still one way in which mink might have harmed the otter population. Mink are susceptible to distemper in captivity, and feral populations in Devon are known to have been afflicted with symptoms resembling it. Perhaps mink in other counties were also infected and had transmitted the virus to otters? But distemper is primarily a domestic disease, having been observed only a few times in wild animals and never in the otter. And, as pointed out before, mink were not about in numbers large enough to pose a disease threat until well after the otter crash. There is no doubt the paws of the North American mink are lily-white as far as the otter crisis was concerned.

In 1971, the Ministry of Agriculture, Fisheries & Food decided to call off all attempts to exterminate the mink from the British landscape. The 'voracious' mustelid had been dubbed a menace to fish stocks, game birds, poultry and wildfowl, but years of poisoning, shooting and trapping had failed to reduce mink numbers; no sooner was a length of river emptied of them than an influx of migrants would refill the niche. The mink won all the battles in the war to become a naturalised member of the British fauna, another of the growing elite of exotics now flourishing in this country: the coypu from Argentina, the muntjac from South China and the red-necked wallaby from Australia, to name but a few. The survivor was here to stay. But with the reassuring findings of Erlinge and others, otter conservationists now had little reason to fear the mink's success. There was, on the other hand, every reason to voice concern over the tenacious sport of otter hunting.

11
Otter Hunting

Ah, there once more he vents!
See, that bold Hound has seiz'd him; down they sink,
Together lost: but soon he shall repent
His rash assault. See there escap'd, he flies
Half-drowned, and clambers up the slipp'ry bank
With ooze and blood distained. Again he vents;
Again the crowd attack. That spear has pierc'd
His neck.

If it did not evoke such feelings of abhorrence for the pain inflicted on the otter, William Somerville's description of an otter hunt in the early 1700s would read like a commentator's tirade at the Doncaster races. He obviously thought nothing wrong with it and simply wanted to convey the belting pace and tense excitement of a sport that was enjoyed by the aristocracy as early as the twelfth century when King John (1199–1216) was reputed to have kept a pack of otter hounds. Otter hunting in those bygone days was great for an outing in the fresh air but it was not half as popular then as hunting for hare, foxes, deer and badgers, and was confined to the summer when the close season for the other game had come round.

Requiring a pack of properly trained and well-fed hounds and a retinue of helpers, hunting was a pastime for the wealthy gentry. Gentlemen of the day would keep a variety of packs to hunt each of the different mammals. For example, William Somerville of Edstone Hall was not only adept at writing macabre verse about otter hunting, he also owned twelve fox hounds, ten otter hounds and a number of harriers. Squire Hastings of Woodlands in Dorset was a keen hunter for more than sixty years and he kept deer hounds in addition to all the others. True-blue otter hounds were a large, aggressive breed of dog from Wales, 24-6in (60-6cm) at the shoulder, weighing up to 65lb (29kg). Like the otter's, their coats were double-layered; usually blue-white they were sometimes black and tan, and they had webbed feet. Quite different in appearance from the short-coated fox and deer hounds from the north, they were aces at their jobs but it was a lucky man who owned a pack and most hunters had to make do with less. Some gentlemen went hunting with three breeds of dog: the otter's scent trail was traced to the holt by sensitive-nosed southern hounds who could pick up smells on the surface of the water, terriers killed the animal and lurchers disposed of it with their snapping jaws.

Hunting in the 1600s and 1700s required no small degree of physical stamina: most were carried out on foot and could last all day. How-ever, at least a few of them used horses: two of the several woodcuts depicting otter hunts show men on horseback, and Bell attended a hunt in 1796 that employed 'horsemen as well as footmen'. 'Vulgars' from the surrounding villages looked upon the colourful retinue as a bit of excitement that brightened up their otherwise humdrum lives; many would join in and follow the chase over stream and marsh. Otter hunting around this time was not invariably motivated by sport. Farmers felt they had to protect their grain and domestic animals from the pillaging bowsons, and privileged fish-pond owners regarded them as a menace to be destroyed. A well-known freelance otter hunter, a Mr Whitaker (c1710–1794) of Auckley, was—according to C. A. Howes' researches on otter hunting in Yorkshire—'a master in the use of the otter spear, and delighted in recounting his . . . exploits'. By all accounts, Mr Whitaker and his young companion Robert Lee were responsible for wiping out a good part of the otter population in Doncaster and its environs, especially where there were ornamental lakes and ponds to be protected from attack. 'Every hall and mansion of consequence in the neighbourhood received him . . . the more he protected the "Stew ponds", the more cordial were his receptions.'

The late 1700s brought a recession to the more popular forms of hunting in Britain. Many of the lesser nobles sank into bad times and were forced to get rid of their hounds. Harriers and fox hounds were the first to go, as they were the most expensive to maintain, but most otter-hound packs were retained and the sport rose to prominence as the other forms of hunt fell from grace. One badly affected landowner

157

was supposed to have become 'so poor that he could scarcely keep himself and his family', but he still managed to feed six otter hounds and one crossbred bull terrier! Such were the priorities of the day—to have no hunting hounds was to be a nobody. The Georgian era saw a peak in otter hunting, and, in chronicling the decline of the otter in South Yorkshire, C. J. Howes tells how the sport became so popular that it supported a keen demand for trophy preservers. There were twenty-eight taxidermy practices in South Yorkshire alone during the early 1800s. Naturalist and collector, Hugh Reid of Doncaster, was one of the many taxidermists who catered for the hunting clientèle. Some of the largest otter specimens ever hounded in Yorkshire were preserved and stuffed by Reid's well frequented parlour.

In the second half of the 1800s, the sport lost popularity, only to recover again at the turn of the century when the hunting infrastructure was completely reorganised. Up until the 1890s, otter hunts had been private gatherings between friends and neighbours or tenants of the land. The Master of the Hunt was the owner of the hounds and invited whomsoever he wished. But the resurgence of otter hunting in the early 1900s brought changes, and hunts were streamlined into regional clubs, supported by subscriptions from interested members. The sport did not exactly widen its scope to include any Tom, Dick or Harry, but it became a little less exclusive. The subscriptions helped to pay for the maintainance of the hounds, the organisation of each hunt and the meetings, balls and other social occasions. At the beginning of this century, there were twenty-one such otter hunts active in Britain, but, over the years, rising costs and waning interest brought the number down to twelve in 1957 and nine in 1976. In Scotland, where the otter is at its densest, only one pack remains in operation. It is strange that the one place in Britain which boasts a fairly healthy community of otters has the fewest hunts, but we should be thankful for this small mercy. Eire had ten packs of otter hounds in 1900 but now has only two. Besides the recognised otter hunts, there were a few 'ghost' hunts (three in 1977), which owned no packs of their own and existed only as Hunt Associations or Committee Hunts that invited active hunts to scout the rivers in their district once or twice a season. Similar exchange visits were also arranged, from time to time, between the established hunts.

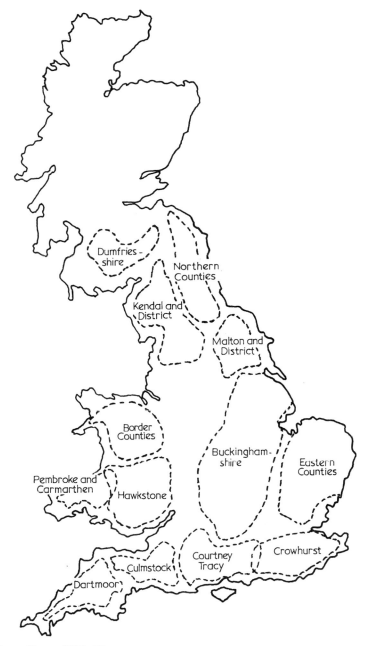

22   Otter Hunts 1950–76

159

Only a few years ago an otter hunt was little different from those of Henry Williamson's day, that is, in the 1920s. Williamson was the author of that classic book, *Tarka the Otter*, the film of which was made in 1978, more than fifty years after the book was first published. Otter hunting started in April and finished at the end of September, and, during the season, each pack would meet two or three times a week, clocking up a total of about forty-four hunts. In the introduction to the 1978 edition, Williamson's brother, Richard, recalls Henry's first encounter with an otter hunt in 1923:

> Dressed in white breeches, blue cloth coats, white ties and worsted stockings, with grey bowler hats and heavy boots, the half dozen or so members and staff of the Cheriton Otter Hunt with tweed-clad friends, family and followers, walked along the banks following a pack of hounds who quested the shallows and root strongholds where otters were to be found. Most people gripped a five- or six-foot pole which helped them to steady the foothold when—as often occurred—the river had to be crossed, often up to waist level. Many poles, the author noted, were nicked with cuts at their top, showing the number of kills witnessed by that individual. One was affixed with small silver bands along one third of its length, each band being engraved with the place, weight and sex of the kill. This belonged to William Henry Rogers, the Master of the Hunt.

Every hunt had its own distinctive uniform with its particular style and colours. The Master was in charge of the entire operation, overseeing the work of the hounds and directing the members and huntsmen during the chase. The control of the thirty-odd hounds was the job of the Whip who got his name from the long whip used to encourage the pack. Hunts have always been expensive to run, and many packs disbanded over the years as costs rose. Richard Williamson recalls how, in the 1920s, six hundred pounds were needed to cover staff wages and hound upkeep, the equivalent figure today being considerably more than ten times that amount. Most of the finance came from subscriptions and donations, but the rest had to be made up on the day of the hunt, when the secretary would take round the cap.

Expensive a hunt may have been, but it was far more costly for the hunted. The otter paid with his life, and stood little chance of escaping

On the look-out

once he was marked down for the chase. The Master of the Hunt would use his own experience and information gathered from the locals on the likeliest places to start. A few seal prints or wedgin spraint provided a clue to the otter's general whereabouts, and then it was left up to the hounds to seek out and follow the drag, or scent trail, of the quarry. Unfortunately for a mustelid like the otter, its smell is so powerful that well trained hounds can pick up trails as old as two or three days, and they will pursue the invisible pathways until they locate their quarry.

During an otter hunt, once the prey is sighted, it is made to swim for its life and this it attempts to do with every breath and muscle it can muster, but, with the odds stacked against it, it seldom wins. Exhausted, the otter may take refuge in one of its holts along the bank in the naive belief that it will be safe from the baying pack. But, to a band of hunters, the deepest of burrows is more an entertaining challenge than a dead-end. They take with them a couple of terriers, which are ordered down the hole and directed to vent the otter by biting it. Should this fail to do the trick, the hunters deploy their back-up tactic of banging and prodding the earth with poles in an attempt to frighten the poor creature out. Sometimes, even this does not have the desired effect, and so paraffin may be poured down the entrance or picks and shovels used to unearth the petrified animal. In the old days, the procedure was guaranteed success by nets placed over the underwater exit of the holt. The otter was then bolted by sending the terriers down the above-water entrance, or by installing a few home-made explosives, especially where the holt was particularly long or difficult to get at. Nets were discontinued in the early 1900s (except in the west of England) though it is not known exactly why. It may have been to avoid the unintentional destruction of any cubs inside the holt with their mother, even though otters less than three months old would stand little chance of surviving alone anyway. More likely than not, nets were abandoned in order to give the otter 'a sporting chance' and so prolong the enjoyment of the chase. Henry Williamson gives a discomfiting description of what is must have been like at the receiving end:

> . . . a pole was thrust into the holt and prodded about blindly. It slid out again. Tarka saw boots and hands and the face of a terrier (which) crept nearer to him, yapping with head stretched forward.

Tarka managed to escape from this particular incident unmolested, but, for many other otters, escape into the river is only the beginning of a very long and frightening experience. Far from being disappointed, the hunters then look forward to an 'exciting' chase through the river. The otter's route is easy to follow because it leaves a trail of bubbles known in hunting circles as the chain, and its position is confirmed whenever it surfaces for air. Eventually, the harried swimmer can travel no further and climbs onto the bank in surrender, too sodden and weary to respond any longer to its survival instincts. The chase often lasts for several hours, and sometimes much longer, as in 1962, when the North Yorkshire Otterhounds pursued an adult female for a whole eight hours and twenty minutes. The grand finale of an otter hunt is the kill, not a quick clean end, but an agonisingly slow affair in which the dogs leap onto their reward like a rugby scrum gone berserk. Some of them go for their victim's throat, while the others tear its body to pieces, and, because otter skin is thick, the process takes a little while. As soon as the otter is dead, the hounds are called off to preserve the head (mask), potter (tail), and pads (feet) for stuffing as trophies. The dead animal is then weighed on a spring balance; the trophies are cut off and distributed to guests and hunt members. What remains is left for the dogs.

In the old days, otters were finished off rather differently, with trident spears or with single-pointed barbed spears called otter-grains. The hunted animal, probably already wounded by the hounds and on the verge of collapse, would suffer the final agony of being impaled by one of the huntsmen. The practice was discontinued in 1896, but William Somerville's graphic account of 1735 reminds us of what it must have been like, though he portrays the climactic scene as more exciting than abhorrent:

Lo! to yon sedgy bank
He creeps disconsolate; his numerous foes
Surround him, hounds and men. Pierc'd through and through
On pointed spears they lift him high in the air;
Wriggling he hangs, and grins and bites in vain.

By no stretch of indifference could this be regarded as a painless death, and the hunts that followed the 1896 ruling were only marginally more humane. In fact, the cruelty of otter hunting was conceded as early as 1951 by the Home Office's appointed Committee on Cruelty to Wild Animals. Paragraph 316 dealt with the otter in relation to hunting and concluded that 'Hunting does undoubtedly involve suffering for the otter, and the degree of it is rather greater than in most other field sports.' Yet they continued to say that they did not think the suffering involved was sufficient to warrant the banning of the sport. As recently as 1977, the then Chairman of the Eastern Counties Otter Hounds denied there was any cruelty involved, going as far as saying that otters enjoyed matching their wits against the hounds.

There were many objectors to this attitude. Animal welfare organisations, such as the League against Cruel Sports, joined forces with worried conservationists to gain more muscle in a new anti-hunt campaign. The national surveys of 1969 and 1974 showed that otter numbers were in serious decline and whilst it was never thought that hunting had *caused* the slump, conservationists realised that the effect of any negative factor is magnified when it acts on a waning population. A total average kill of 178 otters every year between 1958 and 1963 was a substantial chunk out of an endangered, slow-breeding community. Whereas, before, otters seemed able to absorb hunting mortality and still keep their numbers on an even keel, in the mid-1950s 'culling' started to have an effect.

It was the hunts' own figures that gave the first indication of a drop in otter numbers. They showed a fall of 75 per cent in the number of otters killed between 1957 and 1966—at the beginning of this period it took only five hunting days to kill two animals, whereas, in 1966, as many as eight hunting days were required to dispose of one. Some hunts had to close down because of the local scarcity of otters, and those that remained did not find it worthwhile to hunt as often as they used to. In 1950, when there were more than a dozen hunts operating, each hunt spent roughly 50 days in the season out on the chase compared with only 24 days in 1976. Further evidence came to light with the publication of Chanin and Jefferies' paper in 1978. They found that hunting had begun to have an effect on otter numbers *before* the big decline, as, between 1950 and 1955, numbers were affected much more in those areas where hunts killed a large proportion of their otter finds than in those areas where hunts killed less than 50 per cent of the otters they cornered. In fact, the four northernmost otter hunts (Border Counties, Dumfriesshire, Kendal and District, and Northern Counties), where the decline was least severe, had the lowest total of kills for the 1950–55 period.

A serious objection to otter hunting was the lack of any close season for pregnant bitches. Clearly, there could not be one because the otter in Britain breeds all year round. Thus, a hunted bitch is quite likely to be leaving behind a litter of unweaned cubs. 'Even in the blood-sport code in which I was brought up,' argued Maxwell, 'this can hardly be called a sporting risk.' The huntsmen were quick to assure those concerned that pregnant or lactating bitches leave no scent and cannot therefore be tracked; and, in any case, that they could tell a pregnant bitch from a distance and always called off the hounds in time. There is no evidence whatever for the first claim and the second one is certainly untrue. In Philip Wayre's experience, it is impossible to tell if a *captive* bitch is pregnant until about 2-3 weeks before she gives birth, never mind a wild one glimpsed from a distance. The sister-in-law of the Dowager Lady Aberconway gave up otter hunting after seeing what was not recognised as a pregnant bitch drop her cubs prematurely and wait, exhausted, to be overpowered by the dogs. That particular female had been hounded to collapse, but a mother otter cornered in her holt is a force to contend with. She will do her utmost to defend her little ones, snarling and lashing out at dogs and men. Stephens mentions how more than one hound has been pulled under water by an otter and drowned. There is a belief going back to Aristotle's day which claims that once an otter bites, it will not let go until it hears a bone crack. To protect themselves, the old hunters used to put a clay pipe down each of their stockings in the hope that if an otter bit them it would hear the pipe break and let go.

But it was always the men and dogs who were the more powerful. In 1964, this control took on a more positive note. The huntsmen responded to the pleas of the conservationists by instigating a new policy of calling off the hounds as soon as an otter was cornered. The measure resulted in many fewer kills, and the criterion of success for an otter hunt shifted from the number of kills in a season to the number of finds. In the decade that followed, out of an annual average of 100 otters found, only ten were killed. Whether or not the policy had any substantial effect in slowing down the otter decline is difficult to say. There *was* a slight increase in otters found after 1964 but this could easily have been due to various biases in data interpretation which Chanin and Jefferies discuss in their paper. Very possibly, the no-kill agreement had a minimal restorative effect. The Culmstock Otter Hunt suffered as badly as the other hunts in 1958 even though they had made an independent decision in *1952* to kill 35 per cent fewer otters. The decision was made six years before the downward trend appeared, and should, by all good reasoning, have helped to decelerate the otter crash.

Calling off the hounds did reduce much of the physical cruelty involved in hunting, but the chase itself continued to have a very disturbing influence on the stress-sensitive mammal. If an otter managed to survive being chilled by a protracted confinement to the water, its territorial activities would still be disrupted, causing it to remain out of the area for weeks after the hunt. In the late sixties the whole issue of otter hunting began to hot up. Both sides furiously defended their positions and extensive news coverage kept the pot on the boil for several years. There is no doubt that the heat generated did much to publicise the otter's cause and to accelerate the law-making machinery. (For a summary of the arguments for and against otter hunting, see Appendix 4.)

On the 13 May 1969, Dr Edwin Brooks, Senior Lecturer in Geography at the University of Liverpool and former MP for Bebington, Cheshire, introduced the Protection of Otters Bill in the House of Commons. The Bill passed its first reading without any opposition, but it never saw the Statute Book due to objections from certain MPs. 'Quite literally,' wrote a frustrated Dr Brooks, 'one person can block the wishes of the rest of the House—and there is no remedy unless the Government finds time for the Bill to be debated fully, and properly voted upon.' This eventually happened, but not without further turmoil. Represented by the Masters of Otterhounds Association and the British Field Sports Society, the otter hunters dug in their heels and resolutely defended their case against legal prohibition. The conservationists, comprising a number of individuals and organisations (for example, Friends of the Earth, Fauna Preservation Society, Nature Conservancy Council, League Against Cruel Sports and the Society for the Promotion of Nature Conservation), pursued their objective with equal zeal. The two sides became well and truly polarised, with evenly matched influential backing.

The Department of the Environment announced in November 1977 that, following a cooperative survey by the NCC and other conservation organisations, the Government had been recommended to add the otter to the list of protected animals. Several MPs in the House of Commons objected to the Order, the most significant being the Chairman of the British Field Sports Society, but it was passed on a majority vote. Still to come, though, was the decisive House of Lords debate on 6 December. After an intense cross-fire of arguments, the end of the day saw the otter protectors victorious, and on 1 January 1978, the otter was added to Schedule I of the list of animals protected in England and Wales under the 1975 Conservation of Wild

Creatures and Wild Plants Act. However, the decree does not automatically outlaw otter hunting in these two countries. If the hunts claim they are not attempting to kill or injure the otter they may escape prosecution. Moreover, hunts have now turned their attention to mink and coypu, both of which occupy the same habitat as the otter in many regions of England and Wales. Justifiable as the culling of these two species may be, it causes equally bad disturbance of the otter. As Philip Wayre rightly indicates, it is impossible for a huntsman to know what scent trail his hounds are following until the quarry is actually seen, so the chance of an otter being hunted remains, with all the stress that it involves. 'Even if not illegal, nobody could suggest that this would be within the spirit of the law.'

Otters in Scotland and Ireland can still be hunted, though in Ireland every hunt must have a licence for its hounds. Conservationists are currently trying to get the law extended to cover these two countries which are at present well stocked with otters, but they are also intent on helping the otter make a come-back in England and Wales. Even with the law on their side, there is no room for complacency. Hunting was, after all, only one factor implicated in the otter decline, the ban just one small plus for otter survival. Loss of habitat and pollution are much more difficult to combat. Preserving the otter for future generations will continue to be an uphill battle.

12
Protecting the Otter

Conserving an animal or plant may begin with legislation but it certainly does not end there. In West Germany, for example, the otter is fully protected by law and yet it continues to decline and has all but vanished from its former range of several thousand square miles. According to a report from Peter Röben in Heidelberg, keepers and bailiffs still trap them to protect their fishing interests, while commercial fishermen have never bothered to modify their fyke nets to prevent accidental drowning. There is no doubt that a legal decree gives authority to a creature's endangered status, but only by applying a comprehensive strategy of enforcement and voluntary cooperation is there any chance of making that law binding.

The conservation laws of some countries are less effective than others. Britain's Conservation of Wild Creatures and Wild Plants Act of 1975 (CWCWP) merely protects the listed animals from deliberate attempts at killing, injury or capture. It does not afford protection against loss of habitat, water pollution or excessive disturbance. The only statutory obligation for environmental protection in riverine habitats lies in Section 22 of the 1973 Water Act. This requires water authorities 'to have regard to the desirability of conserving flora and fauna', but this is too loose, relying heavily on individual commitment. Practical considerations in waterway management are allowed to eclipse conservation needs only too easily. Conservationists have suggested rewriting the CWCWP Act, or at least amending it to include habitat considerations, but legal modifications take time and the otter has precious little of that commodity to spare. The Washington Convention on International Trade in Endangered Species of Wild Fauna and Flora (CITES) is committed to banning international trade in live otters and their skins, but, worthy as this is, the agreement has no jurisdiction over habitat destruction and other environmental factors inimical to otter welfare.

In September 1976, the Nature Conservancy Council (NCC) and the Society for the Promotion of Nature Conservation (SPNC) set up a Joint Otter Group (JOG). At the time, the otter had not been added to Schedule I of the CWCWP Act, but the Group realised that, if and when this was done, preserving the otter would have only just begun. JOG drew representatives from both founding bodies, the Institute of Terrestrial Ecology and the Mammal Society. Its objectives went beyond lobbying the government for legislation. The Group set itself three major tasks, the first of which was to collate all available information on the biology, distribution and abundance of the otter in England, Scotland and Wales. The second directive was to decide what additional facts and figures were needed through research and survey. Finally, the JOG team planned to assess what measures should be implemented to conserve the otter, using the information already at hand.

Sheila Macdonald and her colleagues tried to pin down the dominant cause of otter scarcity from the otherwise optimum lowland habitats. They reasoned that although river pollution was almost certainly to blame for the sharp decrease in otter numbers around 1958, it can no longer be blamed for the absence of otters from many rivers, as only 7 per cent of England's waterways are sufficiently polluted. Extrapolating from their study of the River Teme in Herefordshire, they maintain that habitat deterioration is the current 'baddie', the dominant factor that is pushing the stress-sensitive European otter from many of its favourite haunts. It remains to be seen whether this assessment is confirmed by the NSP findings. But meanwhile, there is no doubt that reducing any one of the myriad pressures would take some of the heat off the otter. JOG 77 suggested ways in which the worse effects of habitat management could be reduced, and even recommended tree-planting schemes in certain localities.

There is general agreement among conservationists that Britain's water authorities and inland drainage boards need only compromise slightly to do a great service for the otter, with little effect on drainage efficiency. Some 3.5 million hectares (about 8.7 million acres) in

Pair of otters grooming

Britain are artificially drained for flood prevention and agricultural improvement, and certain operations are unnecessary. Clear felling, the complete removal of trees from both banks, could be replaced by selective felling, without affecting drainage. Angela King and Angela Potter in their *Guide to Otter Conservation for Water Authorities*, suggest that one of the reasons for this over-removal of trees is our obsession with tidiness. Some of us actually prefer neat, bare banks. But probably the main reason behind excessive bankside clearance is the financial incentive given to maintenance gangs. The men are paid on a *pro rata* basis according to the number of trees they remove, a sure recipe for a treeless landscape. Water authorities dole out something like £1,250 to have 1km (about ½ mile) of riverbank clear-felled. The one result they can be sure of is the subsequent need for dredging, mowing and weeding because clear-felling probably does as much to accelerate bank erosion and the spread of water weeds (by letting in light) as it does to increase the flow of water from the land. This is especially true of trees on south banks. There is an adverse effect on fish life and freshwater invertebrates as well as the practical problem of increased weed growth.

If left intact, the root systems of those trees that have to be chopped

170

would provide valuable otter holts. When stumps do not produce coppice shoots (species such as alder, oak and sycamore), King and Potter point out that it would be extremely useful to plant shrubs to provide cover for the otter. Weeds and unwanted bank cover are removed by machine or by herbicide spray. The use of these chemicals is questionable environmentally (their side-effects on top level carnivores like the otter are largely unknown), and practically. Their effectiveness depends very much on weather conditions; they are more expensive than mechanical means when used, as they often are, at 2–3 times the recommended dose; and most herbaceous plants die back in winter anyway, so expenses could be saved by waiting for cold temperatures to do the job.

Draining wetlands for agricultural use, straightening rivers like the Dee for industrial expediency, and dredging and piling for flood prevention are all sure ways of turning good otter habitats into wildlife deserts, if care is not taken to minimise the damage. The disturbance of resident otters by engineering works could be considerably reduced if operations were not carried out simultaneously on a main river and its tributaries. Similarly, lying-up areas would be better preserved if maintenance work was done on a rotation basis. It is also helpful to simply leave intact certain riverside features. Ox-bow lakes, shrub-covered islands, sallow carrs, reed beds, gravel workings and small tributaries may be unimportant in human terms but they are strategically significant retreats for otters, especially if they link with one another and with other suitable waterways. In 1969, W. Bunting and his co-workers proposed that the otter-holding potential of lowland South Yorkshire could be enormously increased, just by the conversion into lakes and marshes of large areas of embanked water meadow and washland adjacent to the tidal Don. Although it is not always practicable, manual labour is preferable to heavy-duty machinery for any bankside operation because it minimises the destruction. The process may take longer but could still work out cheaper if voluntary conservation corps were employed.

Recommendations are all very well, but how best to implement them? Clearly, it is important for water authorities to consult with fishing, recreation and conservation bodies at the planning stage of any riparian project, so that everyone's needs can be taken into account.

Basking in the sun

Several water authorities are already trying to do just that, while others are trying to minimise tree removal and to start tree-planting schemes. These efforts are welcome indications that water authorities are beginning to take conservation seriously.

Recreating suitable otter habitats by planting trees and shrubs along denuded riverbanks is a joint venture between the water authorities and conservationists. The watercourses earmarked for such facelifts are those that have not been affected too badly by detrimental factors such as pollution and poor fish stocks. King and Potter give some hints on how best to meet the otter's requirements. Oak, ash and sycamore trees are a must because their root systems form cavities that make good otter holts. A few interspersed alder and willow help to prevent bank erosion, though the roots themselves are no use for holts. Dense, low-growing shrubs such as hawthorn, quickthorn and bramble provide sufficient cover to satisfy the need for privacy. But it is equally important in winter, when these plants have shed their leaves, to have

172

a good display of evergreens, such as holm oaks and holly. A barricade of nettles and thistles on the landward side of the re-claimed strip would deter adventurous ramblers from disturbing the peace of the neo-habitat. Planting is best done in dense clumps rather than in a thin continuous line. The cover should be extended along side streams, disused canals, ditches and flood relief channels that run off from the main river, as these are valuable otter haunts.

One pressure on otter welfare that is obvious, whether it can be classed as a need or not, is waterway recreation. Nowadays, more and more people flock to rivers, lakes and reservoirs almost all the year round and their activities create intense disturbance in otter territories. Most families in Britain own a car and it is no longer difficult to find one's way to the nearest watercourse and to indulge in a spot of fishing, boating, canoeing, sailing or just picnicking on a riverbank. In response to the influx of people, the facilities for these pastimes have been improved and extended, the result being an intolerable level of disturbance in many key otter areas. The Hon Vincent Weir, who has spent many years studying otters in the wild with a view to their conservation, has found that at the height of the tourist season around Blakeney, the resident otters contract their territory and withdraw from the more popular stretches of river. Only after the season ends do they elect to return to the area. Macdonald and his co-workers cite another example of otter adaptation to seasonal disturbance, along a tributary of the River Severn. Springtime showed an even distribution of otter signs, but hardly had the coarse fish season opended in mid-June when otter signs became sparse. Within two weeks they were scarce, the residents having presumably either temporarily vacated the area or passed through it without marking the central section where the angling club operated. The signs appeared again in their old pattern shortly after the season ended in March. Presumably the disturbance in both Blakeney and the River Severn went on at a lower level after dark as well, in contrast to other recreational areas where otters feel safe enough—provided there is sufficient cover—to be active during their normal nocturnal working hours. Vincent Weir also discovered that when he purchased the shooting rights of the Salthouse marshes for two years and stopped all shooting there, a pair of resident otters responded to the peace and quiet by breeding. But as soon as the owner resumed shooting the pair again ceased to breed. It would appear that otters can tolerate modest disturbance (given sufficient cover), but that in order to breed, they require greater security and privacy.

Clearly, the only way to reduce, or at least contain, the further growth of aquatic fun and games is through voluntary control. There are many people among the thousands of river users—anglers included —who would hate to know that the otter had disappeared simply because they had not been made aware of the pressures their pleasure had brought to bear on the animal. People will accept, or learn to accept, restrictions on their activities if the rules have a rational basis. If boat-hirers, fishing clubs and ramblers were to accept a reduction in the number of river users and in the length of opening hours, there is a good chance the otter would be encouraged back to certain stretches of river, if only to commute through to more favourable areas. The cooperation of leisure operators and the public is essential for general restraint in heavily used areas and for the concept of otter havens to work.

Otter havens have been used in Holland for some years now, with encouraging results, and a good start has also been made in Britain over the last three years. Havens are stretches of river or lake in which habitat management and human disturbance are zoned. Behind this idea is the acceptance that protection of whole water catchment areas for conservation purposes is unrealistic and that a compromise must be found. The haven scheme seeks to establish two levels of protection —maximum security (M) areas where otters are encouraged to lie-up and breed, and less protected (P) areas for feeding and travelling. In some cases, the M and P zones are bounded by areas where protection at any level is difficult to achieve.

Several organisations have set about creating otter havens in England and Wales, the Otter Trust and the Otter Haven Project being the most notable. Co-operation from landowners and other conservation bodies has been heartening. The Forestry Commission has given otter haven status to all the watercourses on their land and has banned all hunting on their premises in Scotland, while the Nature Conservation Trusts, the RSPB and the National Trust have all agreed to incorporate otter havens in their reserves. The havens are

174

established at a local level through special committees who assess the needs of the particular area and are responsible for monitoring the success of the sanctuaries.

Havens are selected wherever the food is good and the cover adequate, and it stands to reason that side streams and headwaters should be preferentially earmarked as refuges, especially if they are

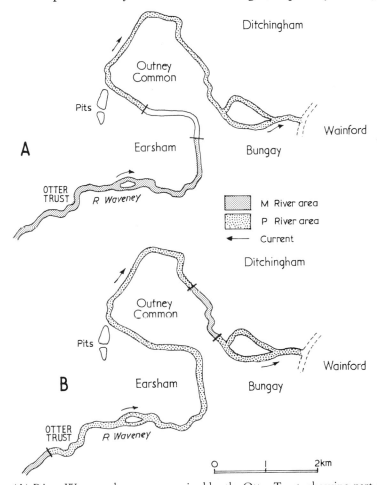

23 (A) River Waveney haven as organised by the Otter Trust, showing part of the 30km M area, all 29km of P area, and the 1.28km of unprotected river
(B) Same area as proposed by the JOG advisers, with 0.8km stretches of M area separated by 10km stretches of P area

175

located in existing nature reserves. At the moment, no one knows just how long the M and P areas should be, or the minimum effective number per territory, but, as an initial experiment, the 1977 Joint Otter Group of the NCC suggested arbitrary lengths of 0.3–0.6 miles (0.5–1km) and 6 miles (10km), respectively. It might be useful to vary the distances in similar environments and, by close monitoring over a period of months or years, to note the minimum effective lengths of waterway.

Philip Wayre is taking no chances. He prefers to see a continuous stretch of river as an otter haven. The intensive use of lowland rivers for recreation and industry precludes their being given haven status, so Wayre has concentrated on the privately owned upper reaches. As founder and Honorary Director of the Otter Trust, he has been responsible for making the River Waveney and its tributaries a complete otter haven, from its source in Redgrave Fen all the way down to Bungay. Of the 37 miles (60km or so), 18.5 miles (30km) are M areas and 29 are P areas. The Trust also went on to make the River Wissey an interrupted haven right the way down to Oxborough. At present, a total of 220.6 miles (355km) of Norfolk rivers have been surveyed by Otter Trust workers Elizabeth Lowe and Carole Potterton, 185 miles (297km) of which have been designated as havens: 165 miles (266km) M havens and 44 miles (71km) P havens. Once work in Norfolk is completed, Wayre plans to replant trees and shrubs in sensitive areas within the M havens and looks forward to the Anglian Water Authority giving the haven official recognition.

Already, efforts have been made by the Otter Trust to determine the effectiveness of the Norfolk otter havens. The 'spot check' method which Sheila Macdonald and Chris Mason used in their 1975 Norfolk survey for mapping otter signs near road bridges, was applied again in a 1979–81 survey. The 200 bridges surveyed in 1975 were checked along with 500–600 others. It will be a great triumph for the otter haven concept if the results show that there are now more rivers in Norfolk supporting otters than in 1975.

In July, 1977, the Fauna Preservation Society and the Vincent Wildlife Trust conceived the Otter Haven Project. Staffed by two full-time biologists, it had set up 43 havens in the Wessex, South West, Anglian and Welsh Water Authority areas by December 1978. The

Nature Conservation Trust has also designated havens in Somerset, Staffordshire, North Wales (in conjunction with the Shropshire Trust) and Yorkshire. Otters in Suffolk should benefit, too, from havens managed by the Suffolk Trust for Nature Conservation. Establishing havens is a slow business, as there are often as many owners to contact as there are kilometres of river. The fact that such good headway has been made is as much a tribute to tireless conservationists as it is to co-operative landowners and water authorities.

Recreation and riparian management are severely limited in all maximum security areas, while fishing, hunting, public access and the mooring of boats are all totally prohibited. Protective measures are being taken a stage further in some counties by the installation of artificial lying-up and breeding holts in M areas. Artificial holts were originally constructed by otter hunters in order to locate quickly otters that had 'gone to ground'. They were designed with two tunnels so that a terrier sent up one of them could oust the quarry through the other. A removable roof gave easy access to the stubborn types that refused to be vented. All sorts of design modifications are now being tried out in various parts of the country. The one used in the diagram is based on a construction used by the North Wales Trust/Shropshire Otter Group. Site choice is limited to those waterways where the main reason for otter absence is the lack of breeding holts. Disturbance and pollution should be minimal and it is best if otters are known to pass through the area, at least occasionally. Slow-flowing weir pools rich in fish and remote side-streams are by far the best choices.

The tunnels which lead to the chamber can be of variable length, around 10–13ft (3–4 metres), though some hunts used to make them nearly four times as long to ensure that the breeding chamber was well above the high-water mark and yet easy for their quarry to ascend. Shorter tunnels are too steep. The chamber should be well drained, built above the level of the entrance, though too steep an incline makes it less attractive to the potential tenant. In the Shropshire experiment, unglazed pipes 300mm in diameter are used for the tunnels, the entrances of which point downstream to avoid blockage by debris and silt. It is preferable to excavate one at normal water level and the other at winter flood level. The walls of the chamber, though not the floor, may be made of concrete, with inspection slabs fitted on the

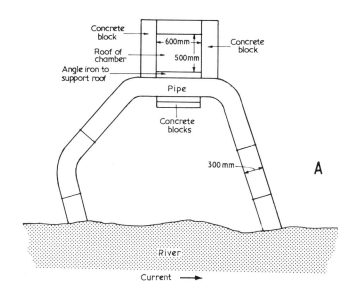

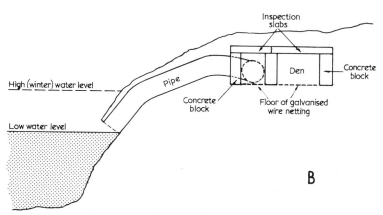

24 (A) Plan view and (B) vertical section of an artificial holt (*After R. Barrett*)

top. Small stones or heavy-gauge galvanised wire netting (25mm diameter mesh) covered with a layer of earth are the best materials for the floor, as they allow urine and wet to drain away. Anything damper than this and the visiting otter may vacate the premises. While the chamber should be free of draughts, it may be necessary in some designs to install a ventilation pipe. Turf is sometimes placed over the roof to exclude light which might otherwise make the holt less attractive to otters, and shrubs are often planted around the entrances that lead into water. Fencing off an area of land and river around an artificial holt reduces the chance of disturbance but it is expensive. In March 1978, it was found necessary to fence off a whole meander of the River Piddle where a holt had been installed.

Monitoring applies as much to artificial holts as it does to havens. It is no use building a holt without subsequently checking to see if it has been used. Infrequent visits are made to all man-made holts to look for tell-tale tracks, spraint or broken twigs. Unfortunately, any visit, no matter how discreet, causes disturbance and there is a chance that otters in the area may be deterred from investigating the holt. Electronic monitoring is by far the better course to take, and a device is currently being tested on the River Tanat. A small, semi-circular disc of metal is suspended from the roof of each entrance tunnel and a clock records the number of times this is pushed. A magnet above the disc pulls it back into its original position once the animal has passed. The detector indicated that an otter had visited the River Tanat holt three weeks after it was installed. Elsewhere, otters have taken up to two years before 'deciding' to use artificial holts.

Philip Wayre questions the validity of artificial holts, on the basis of his observations of captive otters. He has seen them tunnel easily into the bank and surmises that a wild otter should be capable of excavating a holt in a night. Despite his reservations, Wayre is prepared to experiment with artificial holts in the havens that have been established along the River Waveney and River Wissy. Should they prove to be well frequented by the resident otters, they will have merited the money and effort put into them and could become an integral feature of otter havens throughout the country.

It is unlikely that artificial holts will ever be built in the intervening P areas, as human activities there will continue, at a controlled level. Restrictions are placed on the number of fishermen and visitors, on the number of boats moored and on the length of bank they occupy. No fishing or other activity is allowed at night, and ramblers and campers are directed to occupy one bank only, the other being left as an otter precinct. Wherever possible, public pathways are diverted away from otter runways along the bank. In P areas, trees and shrubs should be cut only where and when it is deemed essential, and not just as a matter of routine. Islands on rivers and lakes should be left completely undisturbed, because not only are they ideal otter sanctuaries, but there is no economic rationale for subjecting them to land-use controls.

The ideal answer to the problem of otter conservation is of course to expand Britain's nature reserves and to establish new ones. The present ones cover as little as 0.8 per cent of Britain's total land surface, some of them being owned by government bodies, the rest by voluntary organisations. It cannot be denied that this figure is abysmal and a trifle hypocritical, in view of our exhortations to third-world countries to set aside much larger tracts of land for wildlife. If we insist on building our houses of glass then we must be careful to refrain from throwing stones. The fact that nature reserves are managed with the welfare of plants and animals as top priority makes them critical theatres of modern wildlife conservation. Within their precincts, the authorities have control over habitat management and land use by water authorities and farmers, and they also have powers to restrict public access.

Animals and plants take precedence over human needs and economic strictures, the terms of reference for land-use procedures being dictated by those in charge. The bigger a reserve the better, but small ones, especially if inter-connected by protected 'corridors', can play just as important a role. For example, the Rutland Water reservoir manages sections of shoreline as small wildlife reserves, in which all the usual controls operate.

A private organisation, the Otter Trust, has recently bought its first reserve—47 acres (19 hectares) of Swangey Fen which borders the River Thet near Attleborough in Norfolk. It will be managed by a committee drawn from the Nature Conservancy Council and the Norfolk Naturalists' Trust. King and Potter suggest that Water Authorities should make reserves out of the approximately 320,000 acres (130,000 hectares) of their land that is not under water. This poor-quality land is of little use for agriculture and it would help compensate for the loss of wetland areas.

Reserves and havens are the most sensible places to re-stock with captive-bred otters. There are no recorded attempts to rehabilitate captive-born otters, but this is what Philip Wayre hopes to do with his growing reservoir of common otters at the Otter Trust and the Norfolk Wildlife Park. Wayre started off his breeding programme in 1970 with two wild-caught European otters, and, some 25–30 litters later, by 1980 the population had blossomed to more than 25 individuals. So far there have been no obvious consequences of inbreeding, but it may turn out that later generations will become more adapted to a captive existence than to life in the wild. For this reason, the sooner some of them are released the better, but as Wayre rightly feels, the long-term sanctity of havens must be assured before the releases are made. And the technical problems involved in monitoring the rehabilitated captives must be solved first, as it is no use returning animals to the wild if you cannot discover what happens to them.

It is almost impossible to identify individual European otters by sight or by their pug marks and spraint, and certainly this method is not reliable enough for such an important operation. Radiotelemetry is on the cards, but where on the animal should the transmitter be installed to ensure secure fastening? And how can we maximise the working life of the transmitter? Radio collars are no good because the otter's streamlined shape makes for easy slippage over neck and head, and skin-inserted transmitters could easily be rubbed off when the animal grooms itself. Powered by batteries, transmitters unfortunately have a very finite life, and it is not feasible to add a bigger, more powerful battery, because the weight of the thing is likely to hinder the subject's movements. Solar-powered transmitters may be the answer in sunnier climes, but they would hardly have an application in grey-skied Britain: in any case, the European otter is nocturnal and retires to dark holes or shaded areas during the day, so the transmitter would not recharge even in sunny weather. Until these monitoring problems are overcome, Wayre will not be tempted into releasing his hard-earned stock of otters.

A major part of the otter-conservation programme is the concerted effort by scientists to conduct field research and to collect data from captive experiments. In addition to its distribution and abundance, we need to know more about otter society, the criteria the animal uses in selecting habitats, the factors currently limiting its distribution and dispersion, its range of movement in different localities, and its

181

breeding rate, mortality, competition and population structure. Research into these areas of otter ecology is proceeding and since the JOG reports of 1977 and 1979, there have been a number of publications from university workers throughout the country, the results of which have been described in the relevant chapters of this book. The information will help conservationists to decide how best to protect the otter and it is in so doing that self-inspection must come into play.

Wildlife conservation can easily be subordinated to the sacred cow of human needs instead of trying to attain a more balanced compromise—and these so-called 'needs' continue to grow with our standard of living. There is a call for more agricultural land, on the assessment that three-quarters of the world is starving, but as the starving countries are largely those of the Third World, whither all too little of Britain's or Europe's excess food finds its way, the argument is tenuous. Otherwise, how can we explain the well publicised food surpluses of Europe—the butter, meat and milk mountains? And why the need for farmers to plough back potatoes and turnips and allow Britain's 1980 grain glut to rot in storage silos? Until the EEC has a strategy for distributing food to countries in need, we must face the fact that some of our 'needs' are founded on profit motives and on not knowing when to stop. This does not mean that farmers should take the economic brunt of environmental care—it is a public problem. But they could be given financial incentives or subsidies from government, and hence from our own pockets, to preserve copses, hedgerows and riverside growth, and to refrain from turning wetlands into tatie fields.

There are, at present, a few sources of funds. The Countryside Commission provides grants varying from 40 per cent to 75 per cent for areas up to about 0.6 acres (0.25 hectares) on private land and any size on public land. The Forestry Commission provide grants for timber production under their Basis III Dedication Scheme and their Small Woods Scheme. County councils will provide and plant trees in areas not exceeding about 0.1 acre (0.0405 hectares), as long as the trees are visible from a road or other right of way. Farmers may also be eligible for a MAFF grant to establish shelter belts on farms and horticultural holdings.

Slow-to-act water authorities could be pressured to modify their methods to take greater account of wildlife, even if the compromise is slightly weighed against their interests. The public has to contribute not only materially through taxes, but with direct cooperation if the plan to reduce recreational activities is to succeed. In real terms, the biggest sacrifice this will amount to is having to wait in turn to use a boat or length of bank for fishing.

Otters should be protected, not only because they are predators at the top of their food chain and because to remove them from their niche would disrupt freshwater ecosystems. Like any plant or animal on this earth, they should be protected because they exist. In Boabeng, a small Ashanti village in central Ghana, the inhabitants have a religious taboo against harming any animals in the sacred forest that surrounds the village. By not chopping down the trees, these Africans have a year-round supply of water from the stream that has its source in the forest. The gods are kept happy and the villagers benefit. Perhaps there is a case for such environmental spirituality in western society—it may be the only real remedy for our preoccupation with 'improving the standard of living'. There are, after all, more things in heaven and earth than were ever dreamt of in our materialistic philosophy, and preserving the otter for its own sake is one of them.

Appendices

1

LOOKING FOR SIGNS OF THE OTTER

Spraint Most likely seen as small, conical heaps about 6–8in (15–20cm) across. Old ones may be as high as 12in (30cm) and up to 24in (60cm) in diameter. A helpful indicator on some fairly old sites is the brighter green of the grass growing on the mound compared to the surrounding vegetation. Spraint may also be seen as single deposits on the ground or on top of a twist of grass or mound of soil (see 'sign heaps' below). A single spraint when fresh is a spiky black cylinder, shining with mucus, about 0.8–3in (2–8cm) long and 0.4–0.5in (1–1.5cm) in diameter. It has a distinctly musky, but not fishy, scent quite different from the offensive strong smell of fresh mink scat. Mink scat are thinner, taper noticeably at the ends, and have a finer texture due to more thorough chewing of hard parts. A few days is all it takes for otter spraints to weather into an amorphous heap of grey scales and bones.

The most likely places to find spraint are: concrete ledges or sand bars beneath bridges, the junction of a weir with either bank, the wedge of land where a side tributary joins the main river, sandpits, fallen tree trunks by the bankside, the otter's landing or 'hauling out' places and boulders in fast trout waters.

Sign Heaps Twists of grass or scratched-up soil (sometimes a ready-made mole hill) with a single spraint or blob of scent on top. Obvious only if encountered fresh. Not made by any of the other animals that live alongside the otter.

Foot Prints The difference between those of the otter, mink, coypu, badger and fox should be obvious. Otter tracks are 1.5–3in (4–8cm) long with five rounded toes and a roughly circular outline. The webs make the ridges of mud, snow, etc between the toes slightly flattened. The hind tracks of a

184

coypu are much longer and wider than the fore or hind tracks of an otter and the nail marks are more obvious. Mink prints are too small to confuse with otter prints, besides which the digits are more pointed. Badger tracks, though of similar size, are unlike otter prints in having all five digits positioned in front of the 'heel' pads and the foot is much broader than it is long. Foxes and dogs have only four toes and a distinctive shape of the pad.

Food Remains Not often seen and not left at traditional sites, which makes finding them even more unlikely; left only when large prey are taken. In the case of large cyprinids, the pharyngeal teeth and a heap of scales are the fragments most commonly left. If spotted when fresh, may still have flesh on, but rodents, foxes and maggots make short work of scavenging them. If the remains of a mallard, gull, duck or pheasant are encountered with the flesh eaten from an unbroken keel and with the primary feathers still on, then according to Marie Stephens, it is probably the work of an otter. If the primaries have been bitten off and the carcass broken up, then it is more likely to have been killed and eaten by a fox. In Philip Wayre's experience, a moorhen is treated rather differently by an otter, much more of it being devoured.

In those areas where fresh water mussels are plentiful, a find of mussel shells at specific feeding places on the bank is far more likely to be due to coypus or brown rats than to otters. Neither Wayre's nor Stephens' captive otters were capable of prising open mussel shells and Wayre feels that an otter would have to crush the shells to get at the contents. Coypu and mink gnaw them open with their incisors. Jan Veen claims that otters in North Holland *can* eat mussels and he can even tell individual otters by the distances between the tooth marks on the shells. One would expect that some shell fragments would pass through into the spraint, but none have ever been recorded.

Rolling Places Approximately 1 square metre areas of trampled grass or bare ground (if near coast) where the otter grooms and dries itself. Often found under willow or alder bushes close to the water's edge, linked by an access runway. Characteristic of the otter.

Runways Trampled pathways, about 12in (30cm) wide, on river banks and reedbeds. Mink have a runway system that is similar but much narrower than the otter's.

Slides Inclined runways on river banks or 10–15ft (3–4.5m) long depressions in the snow, where they are often horizontal. Distinctive of the otter.

Holts Usually in deserted side streams beneath the roots of bankside trees, in drainage culverts and in rabbit burrows with an underwater entrance and a well hidden entrance on dry land for ventilation. Those on the coast mainly among rocky screes with a long path leading up from the sea. Temporary holts in tree hollows, snowdrifts and piles of brushwood. Not always possible to tell the difference between otter and mink holts and reliance must therefore be placed on spraint and other signs outside or near the holts to distinguish one from the other.

Couches Areas approximately 3 × 2ft (90 × 60cm) where otters lie up; and occasionally they are used as breeding holts. Usually found in remote marshland areas or on undisturbed islands. Not to be confused with coypu platforms, which are untidy mattresses of sticks and twigs of similar size on river banks. Otter couches are more 'refined', being made of softer materials.

Other Signs Scratched and bitten tree stumps 2–3ft (60–90cm) above ground, made by an otter gathering nesting or couch material. Stephens saw several in Essex in the early 1950s.

Jan Veen can apparently tell if otters are present in an area by small quantities of hair left on bankside plants.

See also Chapter 8.

2

THE WHO'S WHO OF OTTERS

Otters are classed as a sub-family of mustelids (a mammalian family) called the Lutrinae. Their evolutionary origins remain a mystery to zoologists as no fossil precursors that may be considered as bridges between otters and other mustelids have been found. They first appeared in the European fossil record about 100,000 years ago, 'ready-made' as otters. From their appearance in the Pleistocene and Holocene deposits of Britain and Europe, it appears they quickly established themselves as a successful group and today their range extends to almost every corner of the world. Only in Australia, New Zealand, Madagascar and the icy reaches of the Arctic and Antarctic are otters absent. This vast range covers tropical, temperate and sub-arctic climates.

Otter taxonomy is one of the least resolved among the carnivores, some scientists claiming up to 19 species and 11 sub-species (or races), others claiming fewer species but more sub-species. Early attempts to put otter classification into some sort of order include those of Pohle and Pocock and, more recently, Harris and van Zyll de Jong. In 1975, Joseph A. Davis of

Brookfield Zoo, USA, attempted to straighten things out once and for all by taking a close look at their physical and behavioural differences and similarities. Davis recognises six genera: *Lutra*, *Lutrogale*, *Aonyx*, *Hydrictis*, *Enhydra* and *Pteronura*. *Lutra* is by far the largest and most widespread of these and comprises the common or European otter, *Lutra lutra*, the North American otter, *Lutra canadensis* and the 'Chilean' otter, *Lutra felina*, off the west coast of South America. Several sub-species have been named within these three species: *Lutra lutra lutra*, *L. lutra barang*, *L. lutra sumatrana*, *L. canadensis canadensis*, *L. canadensis sonora* and possibly also *L. canadensis annectens*, *L. canadensis enudris*, *L. canadensis incarus*, *L. canadensis platensis* and *L. canadensis provocax*. Some authors give these last five forms species status, ie *L. incarus*, etc, but Davis holds otherwise because they are very similar morphologically and show no major behavioural differences that would prevent them from interbreeding with North American otters.

Of the other five genera, only *Aonyx* comprises two species: the Asian (Oriental) short-clawed otter, *Aonyx (= Amblonyx) cinerea* and the African (Cape) clawless otter, *Aonyx capensis*. The remaining genera are monospecific: the Indian smooth otter, *Lutrogale perspicillata* (which exists as two races, *L. perspicillata maxwelli*, after Gavin Maxwell who discovered it, and *L. perspicillata perspicillata*, the two being separated by 1,200 miles of the Indian sub continent), the spotted neck otter, *Hydrictis maculicollis*, the sea otter, *Enhydra lutris* and the giant otter, *Pteronura brasiliensis*. The giant otter is the longest, measuring 5–8ft (1.5–2.5m), though not the heaviest as some sea otters weigh as much as 80lb (36kg). At the other end of the scale is the Asian short-clawed otter, which measures only 2½ft (0.7m) from nose to tail and weighs little more than 9lb (4kg).

3
ANALYSIS OF OTTER SPRAINT

Only a few spraint are taken from an area at any one time to guard against disrupting the otter's communication system. Some surveyors do not bother to wash them in water, simply air drying them at around 50°C before analysis. The remains are sorted into the main prey categories eg crab, amphibian, fish, bird and mammal, and then each category is looked at in more detail. Most of the work is done with the naked eye but a binocular microscope is needed for the smaller fragments.

Identification to the species level is not easy even with a reference collection of prey skeletons, scales, feathers, hair and teeth for comparison (see J. Webb's 'Otter Sprint Analysis', Mammal Society). Sometimes a fragment can be identified only to the level of 'family', though if a particular species happens to be the only representative of its family in the area surveyed, then the fragment can be safely said to belong to that species.

From a knowledge of the dimensions of known prey skeletons etc, the size of some of the prey that have been eaten can be estimated from their remains in the spraint.

Needless to say, soft-fleshed prey with few hard parts are poorly represented in otter spraint, as are fish from which only a few chunks have been eaten. Occasionally, however, small pieces of fish or mammal skin pass through the gut intact, a consequence of the otter's rapid digestion.

With analysis as far as possible complete, the data (from several hundred spraints in the same area) is usually expressed as 'the relative per cent occurrence' of items, though other forms of expression can be used. The relative per cent occurrence is calculated by totalling all occurrences and expressing the actual occurrence of each food item as a percentage of the total. For example, 15 actual occurrences of eel + 10 actual occurrences of pike + 1 actual occurrence of frog + 4 actual occurrences of rodents = 30 actual occurrences. So the relative per cent occurrences would be: eel 50%, pike 33%, frog 3% and rodent 12%. Relative per cent occurrence is the preferred form of expressing prey items as it has been shown that, in the analysis of large numbers of scats, this method gives results that closely approximate to the proportions of different prey items actually consumed (Scott, 1941; Erlinge, 1968; Rowe-Rowe, 1977).

4

HUNT v ANTI-HUNT ARGUMENTS

Below are the main arguments used in the hunting debate, before the otter's protection in England and Wales in 1978. A labels the hunters' rationale, B the conservationists' replies.

A   Otters need to be controlled because of the damage they do to salmon and trout fisheries.

B   Otters do not eat salmon and trout as part of their routine prey and they are not wasteful; any they do take are the weak and diseased ones that are easy to catch. Otters do more good than harm by eating coarse fish which compete with game fish for food and eat their eggs and fry. Far from needing to be controlled, judging by recent surveys the otter needs help to survive.

A   Otter hunting is the most humane method of control.

B   Otter hunting cannot be regarded as humane. Live trapping would be less cruel and cause less disturbance to other river wildlife. Otters could be kept out of hatcheries by constructing a suitable fence and placing rags soaked in repellent oil at the entrances. As long ago as the 1600s, water bailiffs used to soak a linen cloth in a solution of the herb 'benione' to keep otters away from fish ponds.

A   Hounds are called off before the kill.

B   This then invalidates the two points made above. Even if otters are not killed by hounds, the chase remains extremely stressful to them. A pregnant or lactating bitch is particularly vulnerable.

A   Pregnant bitches or those suckling cubs have no scent, or little scent, and are therefore seldom discovered by hounds.

B   This has not been found true of Philip Wayre's captive bitches, and it is unlikely that wild bitches are different.

A   Hounds are called off as soon as a bitch is seen to be pregnant.

B   Philip Wayre finds the easy recognition of pregnancy hard to believe. He finds it impossible to tell if a captive bitch is pregnant much earlier than two or three weeks before birth is due, especially if the litter is small. In the wild, it would be even more difficult to discern.

A   Otter hunts supply data on the otter's numbers and distribution.

B   No longer true. In 1973 the Mammal Society and the Nature Conservancy Council launched an independent five-year survey of Britain, using volunteers.

189

A   Otter hunts no longer hunt otters, but seek mink and coypu instead.

B   This statement cancels out the preceding points. Even if the hunts do seek only mink and coypu, the disturbance is still harmful to otters. It is also difficult to believe that hounds will never follow up an otter's scent.

5

PRESENT MEASURES

1   The National Survey Programme was extended to Ireland in 1979 under the sponsorship of the Vincent Wildlife Trust.

2   During the National Survey Programme of England, Scotland and Wales, environmental data was collected from each site and written on the same standardised form. This is currently being analysed to help pinpoint factors that are causing the otter to remain in decline.

3   A Convention on the Conservation of European Wildlife and National Habitats was drafted a few years ago by the Council of Europe to give legislative protection to threatened animals and plants and their habitats. Signed by most states in September 1979, the Convention came into effect in 1980.

4   The present British government has introduced a Bill to strengthen the protection afforded to wildlife and threatened habitats. Apart from widening the scope of the 1975 CWCWP Act, it is hoped that the maximum fine for contravening the Act will be increased from the present sum of £100. At the moment, a live otter can fetch a price of three to five times the fine, so it still pays to break the law.

5   Now that otter haven schemes have been put into effect in many parts of England and Wales, the Otter Trust (in conjunction with the Nature Conservancy Council) has started plans to go ahead with the release of Philip Wayre's captive otters. Two large pre-release enclosures are to be built outside the public area at Earsham, and the pools—both 10 × 40m (33 × 131ft)-have already been excavated. It is important that otters bred for re-introduction are kept in near-wild conditions and with the minimum of human contact. Suitable pre-release sites are also being sought.

6   NCC workers have successfully tested a harness bearing a radio-transmitter on wild otters in Scotland. It is designed to fall off after a month or two and may prove useful in the above rehabilitation scheme.

Bibliography

Alfao, F. G. *Natural History—Vertebrates of the British Isles* (1898)

Bell, T. *A History of British Quadrupeds* (1837), 129–40

Blyth, E. Proceedings: Mammalia, *Journal of the Asiatic Society of Bengal*, 11 (1842), 99

Brooks, E. 'A call for action', *Otters in Danger* (a leaflet printed by the League Against Cruel Sports Ltd) (1976), 11

Brown, L. *British Birds of Prey* (1976)

Buffon, G. L. L. *Histoire Naturelle*, 7 (1758), 134–60, Paris

Buxton, A. 'The frost of January–February, 1940', *Transactions of the Norfolk and Norwich Naturalist Society*, 15 (1940), 102–5

Chanin, P. R. F. 'Otters', *Conservation Review*, 13 (1976)

Chanin, P. R. F. & Jefferies, D. J. 'The decline of the otter, *Lutra lutra* in Britain. An analysis of hunting records and discussion of causes', *Biological Journal of the Linnean Society*, 10 no 3 (1978), 305–28

Cockrum, E. L. *Introduction to Mammalogy*, 90 (1962), New York

Cocks, A. H. 'Note on the breeding of the otter', *Proceedings of the Zoological Society of London*, 17 (1881), 249–50

Cranbrook, Earl of, 'The status of the otter (*L. lutra*, L.) in Britain in 1977', *Biological Journal of the Linnean Society*, 9 (1977), 305–22

Crawford, A., Jones, A. & McNulty, J. *Otter survey of Wales, 1977–1978* (1979), Society for the Promotion of Nature Conservation, Lincoln

Cuthbert, J. H. 'The origin and distribution of feral mink in Scotland', *Mammal Review*, 3 (1973), 97–103

Davis, J. A. 'A classification of the otters. Summary of a revision in progress', *Otters—Journal of the Otter Trust*, (1978)

De Jong, C. G. V. Z. 'A systematic review of the nearctic and neotropical river otters', *Royal Ontario Museum Life Sciences Contributions*, 80 (1972), 1–104

Duplaix, N. 'Notes on maintaining otters in captivity', *International Zoo Yearbook*, 12 (1972), 178–82

Duplaix, N. 'Synopsis of the status and ecology of the giant otter in Surinam', *Otters—Journal of the Otter Trust*, (1978)

Duplaix-Hall, N. 'River otters in captivity: A review', *Breeding endangered species in captivity*, ed Martin, R. D. (1972), 315–27

Eades, J. F. 'Pesticides in Irish wildlife', *Farm Research News*, 8 (1967), 4–7

Egorove, Yu. E. 'Relationship between American mink and otter in Bashkiria', *Acclimatization of Animals in the USSR*, (1966), 57–8, Jerusalem

Erlinge, S. 'Food habits of the fish otter, *Lutra lutra*', *Viltrevy*, 4 (1967*a*), 371–443, Uppsala

—— 'Home range of the otter *Lutra lutra*, L. in southern Sweden', *Oikos*, 18 (1967*b*), 186–209

—— 'Territoriality of the otter, *Lutra lutra*', *Oikos*, 19 no 1 (1968*a*), 81–98

—— 'Food studies on captive otters, *Lutra lutra*', *Oikos*, 19 no 2 (1968*b*), 259–70

—— 'Food habits, home range and territoriality of the otter, *Lutra lutra*, L.', *Zoological Institute of London*, (1969*a*)

—— 'Food habits of the otter, *Lutra lutra*, and the mink, *Mustela vison*, in a trout water in Southern Sweden', *Oikos*, 20 no 1 (1969*b*), 1–7

—— 'The situation of the otter population in Sweden', *Viltrevy*, 8 (1972*a*), 379–97

—— 'Interspecific relations between otter, *Lutra lutra*, and mink, *Mustela vison*, in Sweden', *Oikos*, 23 no 3 (1972*b*), 327–35

Erxleben, J. C. P. *Systema Regni Animalis. Mammalia* (1777), Lipsiae: Weygard, 445–51

Estanove, J. 'La loutre et sa disposition', *Mammalia*, 16 (1952), 256–7

Fairley, J. S. 'Food of otters *(Lutra lutra)* from Co Galway, Ireland, and notes on other aspects of their biology', *Journal of Zoology (London)*, 166 no 4 (1972), 469–74

Fairley, J. S. & Wilson, S. C. 'Autumn food of otters *(Lutra lutra)* on the Agivey River, Co Londonderry, Northern Ireland', *Journal of Zoology (London)*, 166 no 4 (1972), 468–9

Fitter, R. S. R. 'In danger of extinction in France', *World Wildlife News*, 24 (1964), 5

Freeman, G. E. & Salvin, F. H. *Falconry* (1859), 350–2

Gerell, R. 'Home ranges and movements of the mink, *Mustela vison*, Schreber, in Southern Sweden', *Oikos*, 21 (1970), 160–73

Gorman, M. L., Jenkins, D. & Harper, R. J. 'The anal scent sacs of the otter, *Lutra lutra*', *Journal of Zoology (London)*, 186 no 4 (1978), 463–74

Green, J. 'Sensory perception in hunting otters', *Otters—Journal of the Otter Trust*, (1977), 13–16

Green, J. & Green, R. *Otter Survey of Scotland, 1977–1979*, Vincent Wildlife Trust (1980)

Gudger, E. W. 'Fishing with the otter', *American Naturalist*, 61 (1927)

Gunn, T. E. 'Otter feeding in gardens', *Zoologist*, 1 no 2 (1866), 152

Gurney, J. H. 'Stray notes on Norfolk and Suffolk mammalia', *Transactions of the Norfolk and Norwich Naturalist Society*, 1 (1869–70), 24–5

Harris, C. J. *Otters. A Study of the Recent Lutrinae* (1968)

Harting, J. E. 'The otter, *Lutra vulgaris*', *Zoologist*, 18 no 3 (1894), 1–10, 41–7, 379–85

Harvey, J. W. 'Lambs and otters', *Field*, 201 (1953), 1129

Heber, R. *Indian Journal*, 3 (1829), 157–62

Hewer, H. R. 'The otter in Britain', *Oryx*, 10 (1969), 16–22

——— 'The otter in Britain. A second report', *Oryx*, 12 (1974), 429–35

Hewson, R. 'Couch building by the otter (*Lutra lutra*, L.)', *Journal of Zoology (London)*, 159 (1969), 524–27

——— 'Food and feeding habits of otters, *Lutra lutra*, at Loch Park, Northeast Scotland, United Kingdom', *Journal of Zoology (London)*, 170 no 2 (1973), 159–62

Hooper, E. T. & Ostenson, B. T. 'Age groups in Michigan otter', *Occasional Papers of the Zoological Museum of the University of Michigan*, 518 (1949), 1–22

Howes, C. A. 'The decline of the otter in South Yorkshire and adjacent areas', *Naturalist*, (1976), 3–12

Hunt, J. 'Note on the breeding of the otter in confinement', *Proceedings of the Zoological Society of London*, 1 (1847), 27–8

Hurley, S. J. 'Tame otters', *Field*, 66 (1885), 776

Hutchinson, A. S. 'Otters in Derbyshire', *Field*, 66 (1885), 742

Jefferies, D. J., French, M. C. & Stebbings, R. E. 'Pollution and mammals', *Monkswood Experimental Station Report for 1972–73*, (1974), National Environmental Research Council, Huntingdon, 13–15

Jefferies, D. J. & Prestt, I. 'Post mortems of peregrines and lanners with particular reference to organochlorine residues', *British Birds*, 59, (1966), 49–64

Jenkins, D., Walker, J. G. K. & McCowan, D. 'Analyses of otter *Lutra lutra* faeces from Deeside, Northern Scotland', *Journal of Zoology (London)*, 187 no 2 (1979), 235–44

King, A., Ottaway, J. & Potter, A. *The Declining Otter. A Guide to its Conservation* (1976), Friends of the Earth, Somerset

King, A. & Potter, A. *A Guide to Otter Conservation for Water Authorities*, Vincent Wildlife Trust (1980)

Kirk, C. 'Cream-coloured otter', *Annals of Scottish Natural History*, 12 (1903), 117

Kruuk, H. & Hewson, R. 'Spacing and foraging of otters, *Lutra lutra*, in a marine habitat', *Journal of Zoology (London)*, 185 no 2 (1978), 205–12

Laidler, E. 'Summary of preliminary study of the giant otter, *Pteronura brasiliensis*, in Guyana', unpublished (1979)

—— 'Notes on the second stage of a study of the giant otter, *Pteronura brasiliensis*, in Guyana', unpublished (1980)

Lancum, F. H. 'Wild mammals and the land', *Bulletin of the Ministry of Agriculture, Fisheries and Food, London*, no 150 (1951), 14–16

League Against Cruel Sports Ltd. *Otters in Danger* (1977)

Lee, R. B. 'The breeding time of otters', *Field*, 103 (1904), 189

Lenton, E. J., Chanin, P. R. F. & Jefferies, D. J. *Otter Survey of England, 1977–1979* (1980), Nature Conservancy Council, Shrewsbury

Levitre, J. *La Loutre—Piègeage à Chasse* (1929), Paris

Liers, E. E. 'Notes on the river otter *(Lutra canadensis)*', *Journal of Mammalogy*, 32 no 1, (1951a), Baltimore, 1–9

—— 'My friends the land otters', *Natural History, New York*, 60 (1951b), 320–6

—— 'Notes on breeding the Canadian otter', *International Zoo Yearbook*, 2 (1960), 84–5

Lister, T. 'A tributary ode to Stainbrough', *Stainbrough and Rockley, their Historical Association and Attractions* (1853)

Lloyd, J. I. 'When do otters breed?', *Field*, 197 (1951), 1935

Low, J. *Publication of the Swedish Academy*, 13 (1752), 139–49

Lydekker, R. *A Handbook of British Mammalia* (1895), 134–40

MacDonald, S. M. & Mason, C. F. 'The status of the otter, *Lutra lutra*, in Norfolk', *Biological Conservation*, 9 no 2 (1976), 119–24

MacDonald, S. M., Mason, C. F. & Coghill, I. S. 'The otter and its conservation in the River Teme Catchment', *Journal of Applied Ecology*, 15 (1978), 373–84

Matthews, L. H. *British Mammals* (1952), 212–53

Maxwell, G. *Ring of Bright Water* (1960)

Neal, E. G. *Otters. Animals of Britain* no 8 (1962)

Novikov, G. A. 'Carnivorous mammals of the fauna of the USSR, Moscow and Leningrad', *Keys to the Fauna of the USSR*, no 62 (1956)

O'Connor, E. B., Sands, T. S., Barwick, D., Chanin, P. R. F., Frazer, J. F. D., Jefferies, D. J., Jenkins, D. & Neal, E. G. *Otters 1977. First*

Report of the Joint NCC/SPNC Otter Group (1977), Nature Conservancy Council/Society for the Promotion of Nature Conservation, Lincoln

O'Connor, E. B., Chanin, P. R. F., Jefferies, D. J., Jenkins, D., Neal, E. G., Rudge, J., Sands, T. S., Weir, V. & Wood, M. S. *Otters 1979. Second Report of the Joint NCC/SPNC Otter Group* (1979), Society for the Promotion of Nature Conservation, Lincoln

O'Rourke, F. J. *The Fauna of Ireland* (1970), Cork

Pike, O. G. *Wild Animals in Britain* (1950), 87–99

—— 'The hunted otter', *Bedfordshire Magazine*, 3 no 23 (1952), 289–93

Pitt, F. 'The enigmatic otter', *Country Life*, 112 (1952), 922–3

Pocock, R. I. 'On the external characters of some species of Lutrinae (Otters)', *Proceedings of the Zoological Society of London*, (1921), 535–46

—— 'Some external characters of the sea otter', *Proceedings of the Zoological Society of London*, 1928 (1929), 983–91

—— 'Notes on some British Indian otters', *Journal of the Bombay Natural History Society*, 41 (1940), 514–17

—— *The fauna of British India. Mammalia 2* (1941), 267–317

Röben, P. 'The otter *(Lutra lutra)* in West Germany', *Otter Specialist Group Report, Survival Service Commission, IUCN*, (1979), 9

Robinson, W. K. *Beasts of Prey in Britain* (1949)

Rowe-Rowe, D. 'Food ecology of otters in Natal, South Africa', *Oikos* 28 (1977), 210–19

Scott, T. G. 'Methods of computation in faecal analysis with references to red fox', *Iowa State College Journal of Science*, 15 (1941), 279–85

Scott, W. E. 'Swimming power of the Canadian otter', *Journal of Mammalogy*, 20 (1939), 71

Scottish Home Dept HMSO, Report of the Committee on Cruelty to Wild Animals, CMD 8266 (A51)

Seton, E. T. *Lives of Game Animals*, 2 (1926), 642–709, New York

Sheldon, W. G. & Toll, W. G. 'Feeding habits of the river otter in a reservoir in central Massachusetts', *Journal of Mammalogy*, 45 (1964), 449–54

Shepheard, S. & Townshend, E. O. 'The otters of Norfolk', *Transactions of the Norfolk and Norwich Naturalist Society*, 14 no 2 (1937), 138–42

Society for the Promotion of Nature Conservation *Artificial Otter Holts* (1978), Lincoln

Somerville, E. W. *The Chase* (1735)

Stephens, M. N. *The Otter Report* (1957), Universities Federation for Animal Welfare, Hertfordshire

Tarasoff, F. J., Bisaillon, A., Piérard, J. & Whitt, A. P. 'Locomotory patterns and external morphology of the river otter, sea otter and harp seal (Mammalia)', *Canadian Journal of Zoology*, 50 (1972), 915–29

Taylor, J. C. & Blackmore, D. K. 'A short note on the heavy mortality in foxes during the winter 1959–60', *Veterinary Record*, 73 (1961), 232–3

Thompson, H. V. 'British wild mink—a challenge to naturalists', *Agriculture*, 78 (1971), 421–5

Townshend, E. O. 'Travellers of the dusk', *Transactions of the Norfolk and Norwich Naturalist Society*, 14 no 3 (1937), 217–19

Universities Federation for Animal Welfare 'Animals in the wild—otters', *UFAW Report and Accounts 1972–1973*, 20–4

——, 'Animals in the wild—otters', *UFAW Report and Accounts 1973–1974*, 12–16

——, 'Research and investigations—otters', *UFAW Report and Accounts 1974–1975*, 10–11

Veen, J. 'Data on the occurrence and behaviour of the otter *(Lutra lutra,* Linnaeus, 1758) in the province of North-Holland, the Netherlands', *Lutra*, 17 no 1–3 (1975), 21–37

Ward, F. *Animal Life Under Water* (1919), 44–83

Wayre, P. 'Breeding Canadian otters', *International Zoo Yearbook* (1972), 128–9

—— *The River People* (1976)

—— *The Private Life of the Otter* (1979)

Webb, J. B. 'Otter spraint analysis', Mammal Society, occasional publication (1976)

West, R. B. 'The Suffolk otter survey', Suffolk Natural History, 16 (1975), 378–88

Williamson, H. *Tarka the Otter* (1978, first printed 1928)

Wynne-Edwards, V. C. *Animal Dispersion in Relation to Social Behaviour* (1962), Edinburgh

Acknowledgements

I would like gratefully to acknowledge help given by the following: Hans Kruuk (Institute of Terrestrial Ecology, Banchory), Don Jefferies (Nature Conservancy Council), Paul Chanin (University of Exeter), Philip Wayre (Otter Trust), the Librarian (Ministry of Agriculture, Fisheries & Food, Newcastle), the Hon Vincent Weir (Vincent Wildlife Trust), Margaret Woods (Society for the Promotion of Nature), Frank Walton, Arthur and Barbara Hunter-Blair and my husband, Keith Laidler.

Thanks also to Pippa Holkham, Beverley Trowbridge, Bridget Wheeler, Bobby Tulloch, Philip Wayre and Angela Potter for drawings and photographs.

All uncredited pictures are by Keith and Liz Laidler.

Index

199